NEW SWORD FOR MY BRIDE

NEW SWORD
FOR
MY BRIDE

Poetry of Grace

JUDITH MORTON LOEPER

XULON PRESS

Xulon Press
2301 Lucien Way #415
Maitland, FL 32751
407.339.4217
www.xulonpress.com

Painting: Castle by Barbara Dalton.
Painting: Winter Church at Night by Robert Stover.
Photography: All photos by Judith Loeper

Paperback ISBN-13: 978-1-6628-5597-9
Ebook ISBN-13: 978-1-6628-5598-6

ABOUT THE BOOK

A *New Sword for My Bride: The Poetry of Grace* by Judith Morton Loeper is a powerful and inspiring book which explores various spiritual obstacles and bondages that keep many from experiencing the deeper things of God. Using Scripture, poetry and Bible study topics, the author invites readers into a spiritual journey of faith and closer communion with our Holy God. Readers will overcome the bondages the enemy tries to cloak God's children with. Using personal testimonies throughout, she weaves the promises of God, decreeing prayers, and obstacles of faith in unique ways. The power of God's healing grace will allow the reader to realize their true identity in Christ. Be prepared to move several degrees closer to the heart of God. Experience freedom from deception and the extravagant love of Jesus Christ and Abba Father.

DEDICATION

I dedicate this book to the ONE and ONLY True God-
My Lord and Savior Jesus Christ.

I also dedicate this work to the sons and daughters
of the Kingdom of God.

TABLE OF CONTENTS

FOREWORD

A NEW SWORD FOR MY BRIDE IS A POWERFUL LIFE TRANSFORMING JEWEL THAT GOES DEEP INTO THE WORD OF TRUTH REVEALING AND UNVEILING THE MYSTERIES AND SECRETS OF AN OVERCOMER'S LIFE.

YOU WILL BE AMAZED AND EXPERIENCE GOD THROUGH HIS WORD, ILLUSTRATIONS, EXHILERATING POEMS AND POWERFUL TESTIMONIES. THE TRUTH OF GOD AND WHO HE IS WILL ROCK YOUR WORLD!

A MAIN THEME SHE TEACHES IS THE POWER OF GOD'S HEALING GRACE TO KNOW GOD AND LIVE THE ABUNDANT LIFE IN YOUR TRUE IDENITY. THE EXTRAVAGANT LOVE OF CHRIST IS UNVEILED BEAUTIFULLY. SHE THRIVES ON TEACHING TO LOOK TO CHRIST IN ALL THINGS, BE FREE FROM DECEPTION, TO LIVE A LIFE IN THE SPIRIT, TO ENJOY THE PRESENCE OF JESUS, AND TO LONG FOR HIS APPEARING!!

A FRESH INFILLING OF HOPE AND FAITH IN HIM WILL BE IMPARTED AS YOU TAKE THIS JOURNEY KNOWING GOD INTIMATELY AND EXPECTING YOUR BREAKTHROUGH!!

I EXPERIENCED AN OVERWHELMING EXCITEMENT AS I WENT FROM PAGE TO PAGE, KNOWING THIS IS A LIFE TRANSFORMING BIBLE STUDY AND A RESOURCE FOR ALL WHO DESIRE TO GROW IN CHRIST, TO TRUST IN HIS PROMISES AND TO BE FREE FROM THE LIES OF THE ENEMY!

YOU WILL BE EMPOWERED TO HOLD UP THE SWORD OF THE SPIRT WITH BOLDNESS & AUTHORITY!!

JUDY HAS A WAY IN HER EXTROIDANARY WRITINGS THAT CAUSES YOU TO SEE THE REALNESS AND KINDESS OF JESUS

AS YOU RECEIVE ALL THESE TREASURES. SHE IS RELEASING IN EVERY WORD A POWERFUL PICTURE OF GOD'S HEART THROUGH DIAGRAMS, POEMS, HEART FELT TESTIMONIES, AND A FRESH INSIGHT OF HIM AS SHE DESCRIBES OUR LIVES IN HIS FULLNESS! THIS IS A MUST READ!!

JUDY LOEPER RADIATES AND REFLECTS CHRIST. SHE LOVES GOD, THE WORD, HIS PEOPLE, AND HELPS THE OUTCAST, THE ABONDONED AND THE LOST COME TO KNOW CHRIST! YOU CAN HEAR HER HEART THOUGH EVERY STORY, CHAPTER, AND TEAR. THIS IS A CAPTIVATING, EYE OPENING RIVER OF LIFE!!!!

THIS POWERFUL BOOK WILL COME ALIVE AND WEED OUT THE OLD YOU, AND TAKE YOU THROUGH A SEASON OF REVELATION, RESTORATION, RENEWING, AND REVIVAL! THE NAMES OF GOD WILL OPEN THE EYES OF YOUR HEART SO YOU WILL SEE HIM IN HIS BEAUTY AND GLORY. THIS WILL TOTALLY CHANGE THE WAY YOU THINK AND LIVE ON EVERY LEVEL. THE PRAYERS IN THIS BOOK ARE POWERFUL!

YOU WILL BE STRENGTHENED AND REFRESHED. YOUR HEARTS WILL ERRUPT IN PRAISE AND THANKSGIVING!! YOU WON'T BE ABLE TO CONTAIN HIM AS YOU GO FROM PAGE TO PAGE. THE RICHES OF CHRIST ARE COMING ALIVE!

YOUR CALL WILL BE UNVEILED THROUGH THIS LENS TO BECOME LIKE JESUS, TO BE WHOLE AND TO ADVANCE HIS KINGDOM WITH PASSION! JUDY INSPIRES, EQUIPS AND BUILDS FAITH WITH DEEP INSIGHTS IN VARIOUS WAYS!! EXPECT TO BE HEALED AND TRANSFORMED BY HIS LOVE.

ENJOY THE JOURNEY!

—Tracey Weiss
Evangelist/Revivalist
CO-Founder/Revelation 19 Ministries

PREFACE

A *New Sword for My Bride: Poetry of Grace* has been a labor of love and obedience over the past ten years. Jesus is coming back, and my prayer is that He will find faith on the earth – in me, in all who read this book, and in the multitudes. His Blood was the greatest sacrifice for all mankind. Realizing who He is and who I am in Him has been a journey of a lifetime. My desire in sharing parts of my journey and these Bible explorations with you is to help you discover, enlightened by Holy Spirit, some of the pitfalls, obstacles and bondages that get us side-tracked in our spiritual journey. I have traveled a road and weathered the storms and pray some insights will save my readers some years of distractions and oppressions. Jesus wants us to live a victorious life of freedom and joy even in the midst of difficult circumstances. We have a mandate on our lives to fulfill the destiny written of us in heaven; may we not shrink back. Let us get all mixture with this world out of our lives. May our passion be for Christ alone!

The Lord allowed me the privilege and honor of teaching in the public schools for 35 years, at a local college, in the prison and in home groups. Having taught both women's and couples' Bible studies for close to thirty years, I strongly encourage mentoring. I failed to have a mentor during some of the most difficult days of my life, and that is why it is such a passion of mine. I do know now that Holy Spirit was ever present guiding and directing my path through mercy and grace-Praise God! Holy Spirit is truly the best mentor of all. Although mentoring is not a focus of this book, the faith journey and subsequent

Bible studies included herein describe some obstacles I encountered that others struggle with as well. Journaling and prayer were anchors in my life when others were absent, but what a gift a mentor can be. I wish I could sit across the table with you now to share, but until then may these words bless you.

I wake at night with dreams and prayers for unknown faces; now I believe the Lord has called me to write to some of them. Whether you are reading on your own, with a mentor, or in a small group, I pray you will overcome all the obstacles the enemy tries to put into your life and acquire a new sword. Christ's Bride, His church, is rising up in purity and grace to stand strong in these last days. My prayer is that this book will affirm, encourage, and exhort each of you to be a holy vessel, on fire with Holy Spirit passion. I pray you will be and do all God has called you to as you wield the Sword of His Word. May the poetry of grace in your life see you through every storm, every trial and every deception until we see Jesus face to face!

— Judith Morton Loeper

INTRODUCTION

And Ishbi-Benob, one of the descendants of Rapha, whose bronze spearhead weighed three hundred shekels and who was armed with a new sword, said he would kill David (2 Sam. 21:16).

The enemy has fashioned swords to steal, kill and destroy God's anointed ones! God has fashioned One Sword to destroy the works of the enemy and His Name is Jesus, His strategy is the Word of God! It is His revealed purpose and power found in God's Name, character, abundance and abiding! Stop wielding the sword of the enemy and wield a new sword of the One who is to come in glory – Jesus Christ. He is coming back for a purified Bride.

God is our King and we have been chosen by Him (1 Peter 2:9) to influence our culture. He treasures us and has treasures for us (Rev. 22:12-13). Unfortunately many of us have traded the truth of God's Word, and who He says we are for a tarnished version of ourselves, fashioned by the approval of others and adorned with our own insecurities and lies of the enemy. We look only through our own eyes and the world's eyes instead of through our heavenly Father's eyes. Many believe the lies of Satan that bind them against experiencing Kingdom living, palace walking and an abundant life.

My prayer is that those who take this journey of faith, as I share my own journey, will come to realize that they are chosen (John 15:16). May they know they are precious and anointed (2 Cor. 6:18), redeemed for another Kingdom and do not need to fit in here (Gal. 1:10). May each of my readers know that it is never too late (Joel 2:12), that our King directs us (Isa. 48:17), and that we can gain an eternal perspective (2 Cor. 4:18). May they know that they can listen to our King (John 10:27), pray with mountain moving power (John 14:13-14), triumph through trials (James 1:3-4), and are forgiven forever (Psalm 86:5). May the Crown of Everlasting Life be yours!

May the prayer on the next page become your own. I'm praying for you!

A NEW SWORD FOR MY BRIDE

I Praise You **Elohim, my Strong Creator God**, Who has formed me in your image and called me according to Your purposes. The battle of sin and guilt has been long and weighty and I have pressed through hard. I have fought the arduous fight and given it my all. I am poured out as a drink offering before You **El Roi, My God Who Sees Me,** and you sustain me in your strength and might. At times in my wandering and disobedience I have felt like throwing down the sword into the dust of this dry parched land and leaving it there. I have desired to just walk away and leave it for someone else to pursue. But during the enemy's accusations of my unworthiness, You **Elohim Kedoshim, Holy God**, have called me to walk into a new land of Your worthiness. I will not fall back; I will not give up. When I have fear of rejection by others or even by You, You are the One **El Nekamoth, Who Avenges** me, sustains me, empowers me, and breathes new life into my being. In times of fears and doubts, You are the One **El Emunah, My Faithful God** Who calls me friend; Who calls me Your beloved, and walks within me, before me, behind me, and beside me. You are **Adonai, Master over All**, the One who wears the Victor's Crown and I pledge my undying devotion to you. You have called me out of any mixture with this world. You call me anew and afresh to come and receive a new sword from You. You have more for me and so I come; to be restored, equipped anew, to go out yet again and face the giants. This time though, I go out in greater power, in greater anointing and in greater strength than ever before for You, Immanuel, are ever with me. When I have come completely to the end of myself and the crushing weight of brokenness, You **Jehovah Uzzi are My Strength** equipping me in your almighty power. **Esh Oklah, My Consuming Fire,** You are truly my breath and life alone. I will not be disheartened or let the disillusionment of the battle get the better of me, but I will continually rise up in Your joy and Your power for you **Jehovah Mekaddishkem are the Lord Who Sanctifies Me**. What lies ahead is far greater than I could ever imagine. I know what You have in store for me is magnificent and I will not fear the supernatural. I come Lord, I come! Forgive me Lord when I think it is about my own righteousness because apart from You, I have none. Impart to me all that I need of Your righteousness alone to face yet another journey, yet another giant. I know I am precious to You **Jehovah Tsidkenu, My Righteousness,** and that You love me so very much; as I do You. If I should find security in all the wrong places, remind me that my circumstances do not define Your love for me. Enable me to speak life and not death over myself and those I love, as I shelter my laser focus on Thee. Draw me into Your Holy presence **Kadosh, My Holy One** that Your sustenance, grace, mercy, peace, love, and joy are mine. I declare and decree no weapon formed against me will prosper for You are my **Jehovah Metsudhathi, My High Tower.** Forgive me Lord should I boast in any name but Yours. I declare and decree, **Jehovah Nissi, The Lord My Banner,** that my mind and boast will be in Christ alone. I declare and decree that my mouth will be an instrument of Your peace, and my helmet of salvation will guard me from every lie of the enemy. To **Jehovah Magen, The Lord My Shield,** I declare and decree that Holy Spirit within me will be all consuming and the belt of Truth will bind my armor. I declare and decree the righteousness of Christ is my breastplate and guards me against the arrows of the enemy. I declare and decree Jesus has shod my feet with the gospel of peace and many will come to salvation because of my obedience to the call. **'Or Goyim, A Light to the Nations** I hold strong and steady the shield of faith and proclaim the great works that God has done. When I feel unqualified, I pick up my sword, the Word of God, and take the land before me in

the Blood of the Lamb and in His name; that name that surpasses every other name, Jesus the Christ, my Living Lord. Amen.
(Names of God)[1]

"For this reason, since the day we heard about you, we have not stopped praying for you. We continually ask God to fill you with the knowledge of his will through all the wisdom and understanding that the Spirit gives, so that you may live a life worthy of the Lord and please him in every way: bearing fruit in every good work, growing in the knowledge of God, being strengthened with all power according to his glorious might so that you may have great endurance and patience, and giving joyful thanks to the Father, who has qualified you to share in the inheritance of his holy people in the kingdom of light. For he has rescued us from the dominion of darkness and brought us into the kingdom of the Son he loves, in whom we have redemption, the forgiveness of sins" (Col. 1:9-14).

LOVING AND BEING LOVED BY GOD

Chapter I

Dzedo and Judy

*I Praise You **Elohim, my Strong Creator God,** Who has formed me in your image and called me according to your purposes. The battle of sin and guilt has been long and weighty and I have pressed through hard. I have fought the arduous fight and given it my all.*

> *"I knew you before I formed you in your mother's womb.*
> *Before you were born I set you apart and appointed you*
> *as my spokesman to the world" (Jer.1:3).*

WOW!!! Don't you think it is amazing that God knew all about us before we ever knew or understood a thing, before the life that we do recollect, even in our mother's womb? Wouldn't you love to 'listen in' on the conversations that transpired in the heavenlies with our Abba Daddy and Jesus before we came to earth? The Alpha and Omega of our souls knows the beginning from the end for all eternity and He holds us close. I don't remember much before age five, a thought here or there captured in a photo, but I praise God that my God longs for me to converse with Him and identify with Him as Father in the deepest recesses of my heart. He wrote a book about each of us before we were born. It's true! The 'perfect tense' of our lives was written by our Creator God. We live mostly in the 'imperfect tense' until we are born again, but once we meet Jesus we begin to walk into the destiny of our 'perfect tense'. Let me explain:

Perfect tense can be defined as a verb that is used to show an action. That action is complete, finished or perfected. Perfect tense is fully expressed by adding an auxiliary verb like have, has, or had. Examples of perfect tense might include 'has lived', 'have written', or 'have been'. *Imperfect tense*, on the other hand, is a verb form that combines past tense, referencing a past time, with an imperfect aspect of something like a continuing or repeated event or state. Examples of imperfect tense might be 'was hiking' or 'used to hike'.

In light of these two definition, we mostly live in a spiritual 'imperfect tense' as we identify with past experiences, past sorrows, past bitterness, unforgiveness, and past failures. We sometimes 'live' there in a state of "*continuing or repeated events*". Jesus calls each of us to live in His 'perfect tense' because He has "*completed, finished and perfected*" all that concerns us. He has accomplished for us what we could never do for ourselves. He paid the penalty to a Holy God for the sins of all mankind. He took our lashes, our beating, our rejection, our sorrows, our infirmities and illness, and ALL our sins. When He said, "It is finished!" He meant it and calls us now to believe it.

The picture above is of my grandfather, we called him Dzedo, and myself at about three months. It reminds me how my Abba Daddy holds me still. It also reminds me to stay that close to Abba's heart and hear it beating; to joy in what brings Him joy, to sorrow in what grieves His heart, and to pursue what is written in my book in heaven. He is the true author and finisher of my faith. He calls me to live in His 'perfect tense'.

A BAND OF SILENCE

Between the sounds of nighttime
And the awakening of morn
There lies a band of silence
Roused from dreams; reality born

From crickets, frogs, and hoot owls
The air becomes quite still
There lies a band of silence
Before that lone bird's first shrill

Between the sounds of nighttime
And the glory of dawn's new way
There lies a band of silence
Where my prayers meet the day

The darkness pulls aside
And light penetrates its mask
There lies a band of silence
Before my day's first task

Perhaps this band of silence
Was placed there just for me
To listen to God's hushed voice
In the stillness telling me, "Just Be!"

I wrote that poem on a hushed summer morning and I love the metaphor of our spiritual walk within it. Between the darkness and the light we can hear our Savior's voice if we would but stop to listen. Just this morning (Oct. 20, 2016) I was stirred at about 3:30 AM and asked the Lord if this book idea was His, mine, or my friend's, who prompted me to think about it. The clear channel of His voice within me seems best received at three or four AM. Not sure why that is, but I'm sure it has a lot to do with the quiet of the night, the stillness of His whisper, and the lack of distractions at that hour. No surprise really, even darkness flees before Him and isn't that how it is in our own lives? In the midst of darkness, He will cause us to be still long enough, through sickness, anguish of soul, or despair to finally listen to His Truth. But back to my question: In my spirit I heard a definite "Yes!" from the Lord that I should move forward with writing this. If for no other reason than the discipline of writing and sharing that it will bring to my own spirit in prayer and fellowship with Him. You see, I have been writing for over forty years in journals and written prayers; through poems, letters, emails, and words of encouragement to others. Writing, as is reading, is part of who I am as a teacher and life-long learner. It is a life discipline that has been with me for as long as I can remember. If God should choose to use it to impact another life or two, then who am I to say otherwise. He calls me to disciple others, so this is but another venue of that service. So to my Lord and King I dedicate this work, this time, and this call.

I love the song Glorious Unfolding by Steven Curtis Chapman. Basically it speaks of when we lay our head down at night and rest, we don't need to figure everything out, just listen to the whisper in our heart. It speaks of a "glorious unfolding" of our lives, as we hold on to all the promises of God.[2] Our lives do not always turn out like we expected. My life has been like that, but I have learned to recognize all the promises of God over my life. Chapman was right on. We need to listen with our heart as we did when we were little children.

I can remember twirling in my front yard as a child of about five or six, arms extended, falling on the grass, and thinking to myself, "I'm the only me in the whole world." I cling to that memory when I want to remember how much the God of the Universe loves me. He loves us with an inexpressible reality we can only realize as we look deeper into His gaze and lay claim to who He says we are. Everyone knows the children's song, "Jesus <u>loves</u> me, this I <u>know</u>." I heard this the other day – "Jesus <u>knows</u> me, this I <u>love</u>." and it made me pause. Meditate on that a minute! It will change you!

At seven years of age, in the 1960's, I can remember seeing the violence of the Civil Rights movement on TV. I ran to my bedroom window, looked out upon the night stars, and cried to my Jesus. I prayed, "Jesus, keep me from the evil in this world, and help me live only for You with Your love. Why are there evil people?" Even at that young age, I knew that God did not make evil people, but loved us all the same. Even then, I knew that something above my comprehension was at work in the heavenlies. I knew one thing for sure, God loved me and would protect me. *"His eyes are on the ways of mortals; he sees their every step"* (Job 34:21).

Little did I know then the journey He and I would travel together. I was created in purpose, though unplanned by my parents, but always wanted and loved. I was taught as a child to love God with my whole heart, mind, soul, and strength. At age seven, I asked Jesus to come into my heart at that bedroom window, as I beheld God's glory in the sky. I was prepared and taught through the Catholic faith to be His ambassador, but I was trained in partial truths. I was sent out on commission for God without the training I needed; without the spiritual tools, mentors, or knowledge I required to do the task set before me. Between the ages of seven and fifteen, I had several visions and experienced a giftedness in knowing things before they happened, but I had no one to discern for or with me that this was from God. It actually scared me a bit and caused me night terrors and emotional distress.

By time I was seventeen, I found I was angry with the judgmental God I had learned about and wondered if the college scene of drugs and alcohol that I found myself in was all there was to this life. One night in October of 1973 it had been raining. I was invited to a party that I really did not want to go to. There was a lot of drinking and drugs. I had loved the outdoors and all that was good about life, so that scene really depressed me. Someone had spilled a beer on me accidentally, and I was not at all happy. For one reason or another it all caused me great distress and the tears flowed. My expectations of college were swiftly fading into a distant dream. Expectations unfulfilled can draw us close to our Father's heart. I ran out in the rain and went to a huge oak tree on campus. As clouds of disillusionment, both figurative and literal, surrounded my soul, I once more cried out to God to deliver me from the sin and degradation that surrounded me. I screamed at the only God I knew to be, who sat on His white throne in heaven waiting to crush me in His judgements. I said, "If you are real and want me to walk through this world, then you are going to have to come down and walk through it with me because I cannot do it alone." Little did I really understand that is exactly what Jesus Christ had done before I was completely aware of all that His truths meant.

Just as I finished my tyrannical outburst, He visited me in that place and I realized spiritually I was pretty far from God; He spoke to me that night through the glory of His creation. Just as the glory of God had spoken to me at seven through the night sky, He once more visited me. At that very moment, the clouds parted, the moon shone through, and the stars came into view. The light surrounded me in a focal point of grace and I felt in my spirit His presence. It was surreal. It was other-worldly. It was a new reality in my life that God was truly with me and had actually heard me. No one had ever shared the gospel with me as I know it today, but God's love found me, He knew me, and He communicated with me. I knew God was with me. How amazing is our God! This is why my life verse is Psalm 8:2-4.

> *Through the praise of children and infants you have estab-*
> *lished a stronghold against your enemies to silence the foe*
> *and the avenger. When I consider your heavens the work*
> *of your fingers, the moon and the stars, which you have set*
> *in place, what is mankind that you are mindful of them,*
> *human beings that you care for them?* (Psalm 8:2-4).

Right after this experience, I went to see my brother Mark, who lived on the same campus as I, and when I walked in his dorm room door he said, "So when did you meet Jesus?" He had met the Lord earlier, and our spirits confirmed with one another the change that had taken place in my heart before I even said a word. He prayed with me and explained repentance and salvation. Only a God like ours could orchestrate such wonders.

It was only two months later when I was in a major car accident, hitting a truck head on. I was listening to a song with lyrics "Jesus keep me". As a faced a rock wall on one side and a cliff on the other, I crossed my arms over my heart and cried out, "Jesus keep me!" As the crash occurred I felt as though the truck went right through me; I thought I had died.

When I opened my eyes, I fully expected to be in heaven. All I heard was a young boy's cry. He was kneeling next to me crying out, "Are you all right? Are you all right?" My knees were touching the rock wall and the seat I was sitting on was all I could see of my car. There was no roof, no doors, no front end, no back seat; everything was gone. This young teenager had dropped his guitar on the floor of the cab of his truck and had reached down to get it. He swerved into my lane and I had nowhere to go. My only injury was a small piece of glass in my leg. I walked away from that crash and began to direct traffic. This was the first of many miracles in my life that I knew only God could have arranged.

God's faithful presence in my life has sustained me through ignorance and sin. In the partial message I had received, I clung to the hem of His garment. I also strove in my human efforts to do all I could to complete the race as I had learned in Catholic school. I always believed my work and efforts mattered, but it took many years to realize that they needed to be done in complete surrender to God and because I loved Him- nothing else! Salvation is a free gift through repentance and our good works an outflow of His love in us. I needed to learn this. My type-A personality developed and strengthened in the following years as achievement and success mattered more than God. I did not understand God's need to love and live through me was to be in His power, not my own. The next chapter of my life would take a tour through the desert of despair; not quite 25 years but long none-the-less; too long! But more about that later.

YOUR STORY REALLY DOES MATTER

You are probably thinking, what is another story in the millions of humanity and why is it important? Well, stories matter! Your story matters! His-story matters! Our history is part of His-Story! Jesus will use our story to bring others to Himself if we're brave enough to tell it, have it covered by His Blood, and tell how Jesus redeemed us from the sin and lies. You will read portions of my story and I pray they bring God glory. So what's your story? Have you ever attempted to write it down or perhaps drawn it out with the main events, the highs and lows, a kind of time-line if you will? If not, today would be a great time to do that. Let the Lord prompt you to remember. Divide your age by 4 and then write out all the blessings and all the struggles in each time period. Why did the Lord constantly ask the Israelites to remember? It gives us a chance to thank God for the blessings, ask the hard questions of 'Why', and take a closer look at how God really has sustained us in this journey. Testimonies tend to touch other people's hearts at the core of their spirits as the Holy Spirit ministers to each one. The enemy of our souls tells us to be quiet and that our story doesn't matter, because he knows a story can change a life. Jesus' story changed mine. May your story change someone's life one degree closer to God's heart.

Oswald Chambers wrote: "One individual life may be of priceless value to God's purpose, and yours may be that life."[3] Dr. David Jeremiah shares a similar story in his book Captured by Grace about Dwight L. Moody when he spoke of whether or not the world would be reached depends on men and women of average talent.[4] Praise God that is you and me. By the blood of the Lamb and the word of our testimony we will defeat the enemy of our souls.

Let's take a look at a few life journeys found in the Bible. In each one, my prayer is that you will see a glimmer of your own story as I have. God's

Word is amazing and His Truths are eternal. May His Word become alive to you in a new way as you journey with a small group or perhaps alone with the Lord as you proceed through these pages. I hope to engage you in thinking about the obstacles that keep each of us from accepting not only Abba's love but also standing up in obedience to His call and anointing. We will explore the obstacles of sin and guilt, disobedience and wandering, fears within, rejection, doubts, abandoning all or mixture, the crushing weight of brokenness, fear of the supernatural, our filthy righteousness, security in this life, and boasting outside of Christ. The anointing of the Lord be upon you as you seek His face with all your heart, mind, and soul. May you be transformed by the renewing of your mind, to allow Holy Spirit to crush every obstacle by the power of His might.

My ABBA Father in heaven says to me in Zephaniah 3:17, *"The Lord your God is with you, he is mighty to save. He will take great delight in you, he will quiet you with his love, he will rejoice over you with singing."* Once I truly embraced this verse as my truth, I began to experience greater depths of my Father's love.

My friend, my heavenly ABBA Father, is watching over both of us today. He calls us His treasured possession, the apple of His eye. In Deuteronomy 7:6 we see: *"For you are a people holy to the LORD your God. The LORD your God has chosen you out of all the peoples on the face of the earth to be his people, his treasured possession."* There have been times when I have felt as if His hand is literally upon my head, His Spirit completely consuming every cell of my body, letting me know that He is not only watching over me but filling me with His presence. I am the temple where He resides. *"Do you not know that your bodies are temples of the Holy Spirit, who is in you, whom you have received from God? You are not your own"* (I Cor. 6:19).

To be in the loving arms of my ABBA Father is the safest place of all. He takes great delight in me just because I am His daughter. The picture opening chapter one is of my maternal grandfather. We called him Dzedo, as he was from former Czechoslovakia. Just like my Abba Daddy, he was holding me in his arms; I was about three months old. I can also remember when my husband would dance with our son and daughter and sing over them as he held them in his arms at about the same age. I remember holding both my children close and rocking them at night as I sang to them of angel armies, the Father's love, and how Jesus loved them. It is those visions that help me relate to my heavenly Father doing the same for me, and I hold these thoughts dear. He loves us even more than that. When I feel afraid or even a little bewildered at this present age, He quiets me with His love. He says to me, "Everything is going to be alright. Your ABBA Father is here just for you." His words are so soothing to me. They bring me peace. He rejoices over me by singing songs of His never-ending love for me. I pray you share that same romance with our heavenly Father.

There may be some obstacles in your life today that keep you from believing you can be God's son or daughter, or seeing with your spiritual eyes His great love for you. We will look at these obstacles in light of who God says He is and who He says we are. These are opposing thoughts and lessons that will transform our thinking and our lives.

Chapter/Obstacles/Truth of our God

CHAPTER	OBSTACLES	TRUTH OF OUR GOD
1	SIN AND GUILT	ELOHIM, MY STRONG CREATOR GOD
2	WANDERING FROM GOD IN DISOBEDIENCE	EL ROI, MY GOD WHO SEES ME
3	THE ENEMY'S ACCUSATIONS OF UNWORTHINESS	ELOHIM DEDOSHIM, MY HOLY GOD
4	FEAR OF REJECTION BY OTHERS OR GOD	ELNAEKAMOTH, MY GOD WHO AVENGES
5	DOUBTS AND FEARS	EL EMANAH, MY FAITHFUL GOD
6	MIXTURE WITH THE WORLD	ADONAI, MASTER OVER ALL
7	CRUSHING WEIGHT OF BROKENESS	JEHOVAH UZZI, MY STRENGTH
8	FEAR OF THE SUPERNATURAL	ESH OKLAH, MY CONSUMING FIRE & JEHOVAH MEKADDISHKEM, MY SANCTIFIER
9	OUR OWN RIGHTEOUSNES / PRIDE	JEHOVAH TSIDKENU, MY RIGHTEOUSNES
10	FINDING SECURITY IN WRONG PLACES/ SPEAKNG DEATH NOT LIFE	KADOSH, MY HOLY ONE & JEHOVAH METSUDHATHI, MY HIGH TOWER
11	BOASTING IN ANYTHING OTHER THAN JESUS CHRIST	JEHOVAH NISSI, THE LORD MY BANNER & JEHOVAH MAGEN, THE LORD MY SHIELD
12	WHO ME? DECEPTION AND REFUSAL TO GET UP!	'OR GOYIM, A LIGHT TO THE NATIONS

May the blinders of the enemy be removed, and the light of Truth penetrate our hearts and minds in each of these areas, as we look into the light and truth of God's Word. Many people cry out for ministry and purpose in silence. May their voice be heard in the courts of heaven as they cry out in prayer the promises and truth of God's Word over their lives. We will look at each of these obstacles in the course of the subsequent chapters, and dispel each one by our Father's love, mercy, grace, and truth. Blinders and muzzles were never meant for God's children. Today we will look only at the first one. We will then discuss each of the others in the chapters ahead.

Our courage for this journey called life often fails because we have lost our hope of heaven. We have lost the anticipation of our ultimate oneness with our Creator; lovingly embraced in His arms. Our God is quite the creative gardener and His revelations, through His creations, are a reflection of His Kingdom. A garden is where He started with mankind, a garden is where He shifted eternity, and one day we will walk in the gardens of heaven.

But first, let us start today in prayer that God will reveal Truth to you in your inner being. That Jehovah Elohim, our Creator God, will reveal to you how much He loves you.

Father, when we are steeped in sin and guilt and do not know which way to turn, may we turn to You and know that Your arms, once stretched out by Jesus on the cross, are stretched out now to receive us in love. Grant us a new impartation of Your love that we cannot contain.

LESSON 1
SIN AND GUILT

We will start this journey in the book of Zephaniah where our main verse comes from. The prophecy of Zephaniah was believed to have taken place around the time of Assyria's fall in 612 B.C. Zephaniah's ministry warned the people of Judah that the entire nation would

NEW SWORD FOR MY BRIDE

be lost, including their beloved Jerusalem, if they refused to repent. Zephaniah made it very clear that they would be judged prior to any blessing. This judgement was not merely a means of punishing the people for their sin, but also to purify them.

God's Word tends to mirror our spiritual journeys. We all know that the world we live in is steeped in sin, but the hope of the gospel of Jesus Christ is in a kingdom that is perfect. Any trial or difficulty we currently face can also be a means of purification in our lives, a means of bringing us to a place of repentance, faith, and greater sanctification; a call back to the heart of our Creator God.

During Zephaniah's time, young King Josiah instituted well intentioned reforms in Judah, but the King's efforts were not enough to turn the people away from self-righteousness, apathy, idolatry, and corruption. God's demands for holy living seem immaterial to a people who find their security in wealth and possessions. How similar this is to our current society. Human nature has not changed much. You will find warnings in these pages, but may you not shy away from the conviction of the Holy Spirit to be truly found in Christ.

Read chapters 1 and 2 in Zephaniah.

In chapters one and two of Zephaniah, he warns God's people of terrible judgement on the nations and tells of all the sins God held against Judah. Though gloomy predictions of worldwide catastrophe fill most of this book, much like the evening news, Zephaniah ends the book in chapter three by singing a song of joy, as he envisions a time of repentance and restoration for God's people. A reminder for us today to worship and praise God through every storm. Blunt and honest in its portrayal of sin and judgement, Zephaniah calls us to action: Irresponsibility and complacency lead to spiritual darkness, but faith and hope in God still burn brightly in a fallen world.

Though a religious people, Judah also embraced false gods and Zephaniah prophesized the fall of Jerusalem in 586 BC by Nebuchadnezzar and global judgement yet to come. This is so displayed in our world today as many have embraced the lies of Satan, and ignored God's call on their lives. Remember, religion does not equal salvation. A personal relationship with Jesus Christ is needed.

> *For they go up to their roofs and bow down to the sun, moon, and stars. They claim to follow the LORD, but then they worship Molech too* (Zeph. 1:5).

The people had become polytheistic and were worshiping both the Lord and all the other gods of the land. They took the best of pagan worship and added them to the worship of God, but God has commanded that He alone is to be worshiped. (See Exodus 20:1-5) The national god of the Ammonites was Molech. Worship of Molech included child sacrifice, an abominable sin. Since Moses, the Israelites had been warned not to worship this false god. (See Lev. 18:21; 20:5) The people refused to heed this warning, and God would destroy them.

- More than a stone statue, an idol is anything reverenced more than God. What are some of the 'other gods' people today give reverence to, above the One True God?

- Read Matthew 6:33, Galatians 3:7-12 and Exodus 20:3. What do these Scriptures have to say about God?

- God will prevail! How then should we live?

Read Zephaniah 1:6.

- Can you remember a time when you did not ask for the Lord's guidance in a decision you had to make?

- Why do you suppose people today are hesitant to ask for the Lord's guidance even when they are Christians?

- Do you believe some people feel that asking for the Lord's blessing is arrogant? Why so?

- A day of judgement and great slaughter did occur when Babylon invaded the land. Do you think these prophesies were telescopic into a distant future beyond this one occurrence?

  Why do you think so?

  Read Zephaniah 1:12-13.

- Because the people did not search their own hearts, were content with the moral decay that surrounded them, and were indifferent to God, what people group did He use to bring judgement upon them?

- What was the condition of the people in these verses?

- Do you see that same condition in people in our culture today?

_____

Write out Zephaniah 2:3.

Write out Zephaniah 2:10.

What is the Lord speaking to your heart as you read these two verses?

This section in Zephaniah 2 is about a call to repentance. What does God value?

_____

Since God's character does not change and is revealed in Scripture, take a look at the hope offered in Chapter three.

Write out Zephaniah 3:1-2.

- Although this Scripture refers to Jerusalem's rebellion, how can verses one and two (especially vs.2) be related to an individual?

Read Zephaniah 3:5.

- How does this verse show God's faithfulness?

- What hope does this verse promise us?

Read Zephaniah 3:7.

- Why does God seek our reverence?

- How can we reverence God more?

Read Zeph. 3:11-12.
What do these verses tell us about what God honors?

Read Zephaniah 3:14-17.

These verses tell of a Messianic era of millennial blessing and the restoration of God's people to Himself. They tell of God's relationship to us as sole Creator of our bodies and our souls; the one who alone breathed the breadth of life into us, and the one who longs to walk in the garden with us. Mistakes on our part, of presumption, or despair arise from unreliable, defective and partial views of the character and design of Jehovah. They come from our current cultural world view that is not in alignment with a Biblical world view. If you desire to obtain a foundational world view in alignment with God's Truth for your life, *The Truth Project* by Focus on the Family is a video collection that's a great place to start.[5]

This passage written for the daughter of Zion- Jerusalem, is also written for us as God's sons and daughters. What does the text reveal about God's relationship to us?

1. When we come through times of great difficulty, pain, and shame- God is with us.

   - Tell about a time of great distress when you knew God was present with you?

2. When we don't understand His plan for us- God is with us.

    •   When or how have you struggled with "knowing God's plan for you"?

    •   How has God revealed to you that His plan is bigger than any plan you think he may have for you individually?

3. When trials seem unbearable, know that God is with us.

    •   What unbearable trials has God seen you through?

4. Times when we feel "exiled", as the Israelites did from their homeland, know that God is with us.

    •   Share a time that you have felt 'exiled' and how you coped with that situation.

Remember this: The mere thought of you brings God joy and He longs to be in fellowship with you!!!

What does the text tell us concerning His residence? HE IS PRESENT "In the midst of thee"; He is everywhere. He is omniscient, but he will not take up residence in the temple of our lives unless we turn to him in repentance and holy fear. God will not bully His way into our heart. Once we accept him however, He then becomes our strong tower and closest friend. He is very near to the humble and contrite of heart as we search for Him. How precious the thought that God is there in our most difficult moments? He walks beside us to comfort us, and whisper assurance, to ease our sorrows and quiet our fears, even when we question Him in anger. What are the obstacles in our lives that keep us from believing that God loves us so much that He sings over us, or is ever present in the circumstances of our lives? He loves us so much that He sent His only Son to die for our sins and carry our punishment. You can be assured of your salvation in Christ today, and if you already know the Lord, be assured that He is singing over you even now.

#1. One obstacle in each of our lives that keeps us from rightly seeing God's love for us is our own sin and guilt.

Yes, sin and guilt are real no matter what lies the enemy is craftily veiling peoples eyes with. *"For all have sinned and fall short of the glory of God"* (Romans 3:23). This is the very reason we are to turn to him, and ask forgiveness for sin. What has God done for you and why did He do it? 1 Timothy 1:15 tells us, *"Here is a trustworthy saying that deserves full acceptance: Christ Jesus came into the world to save sinners—of whom I am the worst."* And in Titus 3:4-7 it states, *"But when the kindness and love of God our Savior appeared, he saved us, not because of righteous things we had done, but because of his mercy. He saved us through the washing of rebirth and renewal by the Holy Spirit, whom he poured out on us generously through Jesus Christ our Savior, so that, having been justified by his grace, we might become heirs having the hope of eternal life."*

Romans 6:23 tells us, *"for the wages of sin is death, but the gift of God is eternal life in Christ Jesus."* Death and eternity are a sure thing on this earth until Jesus returns and raptures His church. All we must do is accept Jesus as our personal Savior. Romans 10:9-10 states, *"If you confess with your mouth, Jesus is Lord and believe in your heart that God raised Him from the dead, you shall be saved. For it is with your heart that you believe and are justified, and it is with your mouth that you confess and are saved.*" We can allow Jesus to cast our sins into the sea of forgetfulness, as far as the east is from the west, by confessing our need for a Savior and accepting Christ into our heart. This plan that the Father prepared for us places us under the blood of Christ, puts us in right relationship with our heavenly Father, so sin and guilt no longer need to be an obstacle in our lives. Each day we can and should place our lives in His hands, and in His will; to do His good pleasure and not our own.

Just as the verses we read in Zephaniah tell of a Messianic era of Millennial blessing and restoration of God's people to Himself, so too, each of us needs to experience that same individual redemptive salvation through the Blood of Jesus on the cross, and through His resurrection. Ephesians 2:8-9 states, "*For it is by grace you have been saved through faith- and this is not from yourselves, it is a gift of God – not by works so that no one can boast. For we are God's workmanship, created in Christ Jesus to do good works, which God prepared in advance for us to do.*" Did you notice the word "gift"? We cannot earn our salvation by being "good enough". None of us will ever be good enough. Our righteousness is as filthy rags. If it was not for the grace of our loving Father, none of us would be saved. God's relationship to us as sole Creator of our bodies and our souls is one that needs to be truly realized and received by us. He is the only One who breathes new life into us, and the One who longs to walk in the garden with us today and forever. "*For God so loved the world that He gave us His only begotten Son that whoever believes in Him will not perish but have everlasting life*" (John 3:16).

PRAYER TO ELOHIM, MY CREATOR GOD

If you would like to offer a prayer to your Father today, this may get you started:

I Praise You Elohim, my strong Creator God, who has formed me in your image and called me according to your purposes. In the beginning you, God (Elohim) created the heavens and the earth. The earth was formless and void, and darkness was over the surface of the deep, and the Spirit of God was moving over the surface of the waters. Even then you knew me before you formed me in my mother's womb. Before I was born you set me apart and appointed me as a spokesman to the world, to declare your glory and your praise. I submit my life to you Lord Jesus, anew and afresh, to declare the works that you have done. I believe you are the Son of God, Jesus, and that you died on the cross for my sin and shame, making a way for me to spend eternal life with you, my precious Lord. On the third day, you rose from the dead defeating sin, death, and the grave. I put my undying faith in you and long to live in fellowship with you all the days of my life. You alone Lord hold the universes in place, you alone hold my heart in place, my mind in wholeness, and my soul in eternity. You, Jesus are from everlasting to everlasting and I worship you today. Praise you for loving me so much that you died on that cross for me. Thank you for opening all of heaven's gates over me, and being my redemption, provision, health, justice, peace, and joy. You Lord, my God, are with me, you are mighty to save. You will take great delight in me, you will quiet me with your love, and you will rejoice over me with singing. I love you Father, Son, and Spirit. Amen.

SHARING YOUR STORY

Were you ever asked to share your testimony? Sharing your own testimony of faith does not need to be a long, drawn-out dissertation of your life but rather a short 3-4 minute introduction to how the gospel of Christ impacted your life. In Acts 26 Paul shares his testimony with Agrippa. He spoke simply, logically, and clearly of how his life was before Christ, how he met Christ as Savior and Lord, and how his life was changed after conversion. Our testimony serves as an open-door, if you will, to conversations that lead others to hear the gospel. They are not always a convincing tool, but rather an introducing tool to the things of God. A testimony, aptly spoken with Christ at its center, can often lead to talking about the gospel. If you peruse Acts 26, you will see how Paul gave his testimony: Verses 2-3 were his lead in; verses 4-11 described his life before Christ; verses 12-20 told of how he was saved; verses 21-23 spoke of the time after his conversion, and in verses 24-29 we find his closing. If you pattern your experience after this, you will have a concise way to share your own story. Why not write it out today, if you never have, and then share it with someone. Perhaps you can practice in a small group, if you are in one. If not, practice it with a friend who may not know Jesus, and see what God will do in that conversation. God Bless!

Chapter II

*I am poured out as a drink offering before You **El Roi, My God Who Sees Me**, and You sustain me in Your strength and might through every battle. At times in my wandering and disobedience I have felt like throwing down the sword into the dust of this dry parched land and leaving it there. I have desired to just walk away and leave it for someone else to pursue.*

> *She gave this name to the LORD who spoke to her: "You are the God who sees me," for she said, "I have now seen the One who sees me" (Genesis 16:13).*

Just as in Genesis 16 when Hagar was brought to a better attitude, after encountering an Angel who was the eternal Word and Son of God, we too should admire the Lord's mercy and grace in our own lives. Are you comforted today, like Hagar, that "Thou God sees me!"

AN EXPRESSION OF EARLY FAITH

I once was a child
Seemingly shut inside myself
I longed to reach outside myself
Come down from off my shelf

I opened my eyes and saw God's love
I opened my ears and heard His hush
I reached to the 'Son' for warmth and light
I reached out to Christ, He holds me at night

My faith is but a simple one
I cannot see God's plan for me
My love for Him, I cannot always show
I believe in Him, and this is all I know

He's there in my joys
He's there in my sorrows
My prayer is that He'll be here
In all my tomorrows.

What do we do when life does not turn out as we planned? What do we do when our life is poured out, and we are no longer sure which way to turn? After learning how to worship in a little Assemblies of God trailer in Clarion county for three years, being baptized both in water and the Spirit, participating in Campus Crusade for Christ outreaches, street witnessing, preaching, teaching youth, and running group homes, I developed a dream of what I thought God wanted me to do with my life. I thought my trajectory was set; to be a pastor's wife and missionary.

My first love of three years was intertwined with my love for Jesus. It felt complete at the time as we ministered together on campus, but the young man I thought I would spend the rest of my life with went to seminary in Texas. We still planned to marry and spoke on the phone, wrote letters and visited each other whenever we could. But then he called four months before the wedding, and told me that he had fathered a child with another. He was planning to marry her instead. The floor fell out from under me, and I spiraled into a state of confusion, depression and bulimia. After that very difficult break-up and then another failed Christian engagement, I moved across the state to start fresh in a new job. One of the problem was I had no mentors to disciple me. I had been hired to take care of three mentally handicapped children in a group home. At 21, people in this area of our state looked at me a little strangely with three handicapped children. I am sorry to say, we were snubbed even in several churches I had visited. Finally, I decided to throw my Bible across the room and see what the world had to offer.

Where I found myself was in another state, kidnapped by a non-believer who was narcissistic. Beaten and broken in every sense of the word, I was humiliated, defeated and lost all self-respect. I spiraled into a spiritual death of sorts. When I called 911 for help, the young man's father was the police officer who showed up. He talked me out of all charges; I just wanted to go home. A season of drugs and not caring any longer about being pure, the clouds of disillusionment and sin overtook me. This time it resulted in years of depressions, anxieties, overachieving, nightmares, and loneliness. *"Where can I go from your Spirit? Where can I flee from your presence"* (Psalm 139:7)? Nowhere! The Lord was with me still sustaining me and abiding with me even in this difficult season.

After these bad decisions caused me so much shame and self-loathing, I met my husband. How we met was nothing short of a miracle as I look back. One of the children I lived with, in the group home, locked me out of the house, and then had a seizure. I went across the street to ask for help. My future husband came over, and we spent the better part of that late afternoon and evening together. His joy in playing with the children touched my heart. After eight hours, he asked me to marry him. I looked to him to be my salvation from any further abuse, but even commitments in our marriage failed. I knew enough Scripture to know that if I did not forgive, God would not forgive me. I had a lot to forgive both from my past and my current situation. So after a rocky start to our marriage, I consigned myself to continue on the best I could. Whenever we look to someone else to fulfill a need in us that only God was meant to fill, we will be both disappointed and off track spiritually.

Henry Nouwin was a Christian writer who meditated on Rembrandt's painting of *The Return of the Prodigal,* and as the years passed, his focus shifted from seeing the son who needed forgiveness to the father who needed to forgive. He shared a similar thought about looking to others to be your salvation.

Henry Nouwen wrote:

> *When we expect a friend or lover to be able to take away our deepest pain, we expect from him or her something that cannot be given by human beings. No human being can understand us fully, no human being can give us unconditional love, no human being can offer constant affection, and no human being can enter into the core of our beings and heal our deepest brokenness. When we forget that and expect from others more than they can give, we will be quickly disillusioned; for when we do not receive what we expect, we easily become resentful, bitter, revengeful, and even violent.*[6]

Bitterness took root in my life, and it is nothing short of a miracle that my husband and I have survived these 43 years. I turned away from my new found faith seeking solace in Catholicism once more. It was familiar, it was accepted by my family, and it was a cop-out on my part. My strong thinking was that the Catholic faith did give me a good foundation of faith, so perhaps it would do the same for my children. I sought the Lord amid my confusion and grief.

God's Word sustained me as I clung to the kernels of truth I knew to be right. My mind, heart, and soul were out of alignment with what God had originally intended for my life, and I knew it. I was teaching special education students who needed emotional support; many times I felt I was the one who needed emotional support. I wrote in my journals through my entire life crying out to God as the Spirit convicted me continually, and tried to lovingly call me back to His presence. Depression, bulimia, night terrors and suicidal thoughts consumed me at times, and were it not for a loving, patient husband and two beautiful children who needed me, I would not be alive today. My mind sought to know Him amidst confusion, my heart yearned to love Him without complete examples of His love, and my soul wished to be one with Him without the truth of teaching on His Spirit.

At forty-three years old in 1998 a friend invited me a Women of Faith Conference in Philadelphia. One woman could not go, and her sickness became my recommitment to trusting the Holy Spirit with my life. We never know the whole story in all the mini-stories of life, or how God may use our suffering or illness to further His Kingdom. Sheila Walsh was speaking and she had dealt with deep depression as well. I sat mesmerized and tearful as I listened to her story. God began to align my heart, mind, and spirit more and more in understanding His truths. For, *"Nothing in all creation is hidden from God's sight. Everything is uncovered and laid bare before the eyes of Him to whom we must give account"* (Heb. 4:13). He saw me and He alone was faithful to me. His continuous presence in my life today is through continued immersion in His life-giving river; His Word and the Holy Spirit. The conference was on a Saturday and that Sunday the Lord led me to a Bible believing church. A precious elder saint at that church greeted me with a hug that was more healing than she will ever know. Never underestimate the significance of your role in the body of Christ. One act of kindness may be remembered and quite significant in Kingdom work for years to come; even a hug.

In 2000, the Lord began to grow me in faith through joining our choir, and learning how to worship in spirit and in truth. I began to delight in the Lord as it tells us in Job 22:26, *"Surely then you will find delight in the Almighty and will lift up your face to God."*

I taught in home Bible groups since 1996, began teaching evenings in a local college, and continued to teach in the public schools. Since 1998 I have learned how to worship in spirit and truth, minister to women in small groups in my home, at church, and at the prison. I served on women's councils, healing teams, as an altar worker, and as a spiritual coach and mentor. Only a God like ours is able to do all this! He is ever faithful!

I loved John Wesley's words when he said, *"Do all the good you can, By all the means you can, In all the ways you can, In all the places you can, At all the times you can, To all the people you can, As long as ever you can."*[7]

I think he was type A also.

Perhaps you can related to some of this. Sometimes we're waiting for God to do something, and He is waiting for us to do something different. If we want different results in our lives, we need to embrace different goals and attitudes, aligning them with the Word of God.

Have you ever been trapped in a pattern of spiritual wandering, disobedience and pain that you knew was not wholesome? When depression, anxiety, and never-ending doubt consume your thinking, you tend to get negative, fearful, and sometimes even suicidal. To the world you may look quite successful, and just about all who know you may think you have it all figured out. Of course, the ones closest to you see your anguish, but are not always able to offer solutions, options, or words of encouragement and truth. Between the ages of 26 and 42 this is exactly where I found myself. My career was going well, my studies were going well, but they truly were an avenue of escape from thinking about my own spiritual condition. My marriage had its difficulties as I battled the enemy of my soul in the recesses of my mind over past failures, lost expectations, and a kidnapping that occurred when I was 21. It was during this time, however, the Lord gifted me with two beautiful children, and the love and joy I found in them was immeasurable. They caused me to want to hang onto the hem of the Lord's garment and keep going. When I look back on this time, I had numerous blessings in my life, but at the time, I failed to acknowledge them, or praise God for them as I should have. I remember living in the Psalms. Reading and praying the Psalms kept me alive. I'm sure my children suffered because of my anguish of soul but I tried to stay positive for them.

I've always been introspective, but I had no peace and my joy was fleeting, not abiding. And so I continued to wander in the strongholds of depression and anxiety, never truly walking in the freedom Christ had originally offered me. I allowed bitterness and lack of forgiveness to take root in my spirit and grow. I looked back instead of forward, I was resentful instead of grateful, and I was veiled in a downcast gaze, instead of lifting my head to where my help comes from. I still had faith in Christ, but it was not a victorious faith. After all, even Satan knows who Jesus is. Knowing Him and following Him are two different concepts. Head knowledge verses heart knowledge. There were times when I wanted to pull out in front of trucks, and it was then I knew I was in deep trouble. I sought medical help, and got on some anti-depressants for a while. The Psalms offered me an anchor to my soul with the Lord during this time, and I can remember laying on the floor crying out to God to bring me peace and save my life for the sake of my children. I clung to Jesus but was still living in the lies of the enemy, because I did not know the Word or its promises, and was not standing in the authority that Christ had returned to me. I was *at the foot* of the cross but had not yet traversed *through* the cross to victory.

LESSON 2

WANDERING IN DISOBEDIENCE

WHAT SOIL AM I IN? I'M PLANTED BY HIS HAND

Read Matthew 13:4-8. God plants us in certain soils, some nourishing, and some not so nourishing. Faith in Christ can transplant us into good soil, where we can grow and thrive. As a new believer, the Lord longs to surround us with the fellowship of the saints to bring us under Godly leaders. These individuals are intended to feed us on the Word of Truth, disciple and mentor us through difficult seasons. No believer was ever meant to be an island. Isolation is a lie of the enemy to deceive a person with his veil of confusion, mistrust, deception, bitterness, loneliness, hate, and despair. Without godly mentors, it is not a question of "if" we will stray, but only "how far".

Jesus came to destroy the works of the enemy.

> *The one who does what is sinful is of the devil, because the devil has been sinning from the beginning. The reason the Son of God appeared was to destroy the devil's work.* (I John 3:8).

God will destroy all the weeds and bad soil in our lives as we submit to His call; totally surrendering our lives to the One who died for us. We will begin to understand where He plants us for His purposes.

- Give a brief description of where and how you grew up?

Read Genesis 16:4-6.

Sarai gives Hagar to Abram

I am sure many of you may know the story of Sarai and Hagar. Sarai was Abram's wife and was no longer expecting to bear children. She proposed that he take another wife, her handmaid Hagar, and then her children would be Sarai's. No one stopped to ask the counsel of the Lord, and their unbelief in the promise of God's almighty power was forgotten. Seeking God's counsel is how many of us live until we find ourselves in dire straits. This is so much a part of many people's lives. We do not want to wait on the Lord's timing or seek his face in our situations. Rather, we use or abuse his blessings that He has appointed over our lives. That is exactly what I did in my own life when circumstances did not go the way I had wanted. I set out on a course to direct my own life instead of waiting on the timing of Almighty God. I was not patiently submitting in the exercise of my faith. Whenever we use fleshly wisdom of man, and not seek the counsel of Godly wisdom, we will be off track of the original intent of God's will for our lives. So before attempting things that are doubtful, ask counsel of God through His Word and through prayer.

Read Genesis 16:5.

Accusing others

Sarai arranged for Hagar to give birth to Ishmael, but rather than ask God's forgiveness, she looked at Abram and Hagar with blame and resentment. We tend to accuse and strike out at others in frustration when our spirits are under the conviction of a holy God. Adam and Eve did the same thing in Gen. 3:12-13. Anger arises from our own shortcomings in living up to the standard God requires. That standard can only be met under the blood of Christ, who can perfect in us what we lack in the flesh of our own ability. Our freedom resides in Christ alone, the author and the one who perfects our faith. No one is ever good enough nor can they be- we all need a Savior.

Read Genesis 16:7-16.

- What mischief occurred?

- When grief follows our own disobedience, why do people still blame God?

- Why was Hagar upset? How can we bear the suffering of our own faults patiently?

- How did she come to terms with where God had placed her?

Read Genesis 16:8.

Running Away from problems

Hagar tried to run away from her mistress and her problems. Running from problems rarely solves them. Hagar needed to face Sarai, the cause of her problem, and submit to her. It's wise to face our problems, accept the Lord's help, seek wisdom in the midst of them, and change our stinking thinking. I took things into my own hands to try and solve my problems just like Hagar. I was running from a truth I knew to be true, my relationship with Christ over the religion of man. We can run but we cannot hide from the Lover of our souls. He carries us through even when we are not leaning on Him. Consider this:

> *If any of you lacks wisdom, you should ask God, who gives generously to all without finding fault, and it will be given to you. But when you ask, you must believe and not doubt, because the one who doubts is like a wave of the sea, blown and tossed by the wind. That person should not expect to receive anything from the Lord. Such a person is double-minded and unstable in all they do. (James 1:5-8)*

- Can you remember a time when you made a human decision without God's counsel, and it went royally wrong?

- Remember that the Lord gives His children all good gifts, but He wants us to be in fellowship and relationship with him. Have you ever made a decision with Godly wisdom because you sought His counsel in prayer and in His Word, and then found God's favor? Explain. If not, write a prayer asking for God's wisdom for an important decision you are currently facing.

Read Genesis 16:13.

There were actually three serious problems or mistakes reflected in these passages.

- Sarai took matters into her own hands when she did not conceive.

- Abram went along with Sarai's plan without consulting God.

- Hagar ran away from her problems.

I find it amazing that, despite their sin and disobedience, God still worked things together for their good. (See Rom. 8:28). Hagar's problem was resolved despite Abram's refusal to get involved, and Sarai and Abram received their promised son. I too am amazed at how God is working together all things for my good, even though I had turned away from the bit of truth I knew to be true.

How Do We Seek the Counsel of the Lord?

When the Angel found Hagar in the desert, she was far from where she belonged. She was way off track with where she needed to be to perform her duties. Furthermore, she was far away from God's plan for her life. God shows us, as He did Hagar, great mercy when He stops us in our tracks from a sinful way. Whether it is due to our own conscience, or by His divine hand of providence, the Holy Spirit of heaven pursues us because of God's great love for us. Praise and joy should be our only response. Had Hagar actually made it to Egypt, she would have returned to a wilderness experience far greater than she knew; idol worship, danger, and misery. When we remember who we are and whose we are, we are wise in remembering our duty, our calling, and the home that is ours. Just as Hagar was brought to a better attitude after encountering this Angel, who was the eternal Word and Son of God, we too should admire the Lord's mercy and grace in our own lives. Are you comforted today, like Hagar, that "Thou God sees me!" I know I am.

2 Corinthians 4:6 states, *"For God, who said, "Let light shine out of darkness," made his light shine in our hearts to give us the light of the knowledge of the glory of God in the face of Christ."* And in Eccl. 3:11 we

see that, *"He has made everything beautiful in its time. He has also set eternity in the hearts of men."* Just as Hagar was disappointed and confused by the circumstances of her life and tried to run away, God's presence still pursued her. She, however, needed to obey His voice. Never forget that the saving knowledge of Jesus Christ is a gift from God, He lovingly pursues us in truth. Nothing we have done can separate us from His forgiveness and His love. We need only believe and receive.

Has there been a time or season in your own life when you have felt disappointed or confused and it caused you to run from God or others? Have you ever shared it with a friend?

If you remember in chapter one we looked at the obstacles in each of our lives that keep us from rightly seeing God's love for us. We had briefly looked at sin and guilt in chapter one. Now this lesson on Hagar brings us back to look at the second obstacle of disobedience and wandering from God. We'll consider this one similarly in light of God's Word of Truth, to dispel it by our Father's love, mercy, and grace.

#2. The second obstacle that keeps us from enjoying a right relationship with the Father as His son or daughter is our disobedience and continually wandering away from God, just as Hagar did in the desert. When we wander away from God, He will discipline us to draw us back to fellowship with Him. Proverbs 3:11-12 states, *"My son, do not despise the LORD's discipline, and do not resent his rebuke, because the LORD disciplines those he loves, as a father the son he delights in."* I am so grateful the Lord loved me enough to discipline me, drawing me back to Himself. I praise God that His Holy Spirit brought illumination to my mind and clarity to my spirit to give me wisdom. I believe the season of doubt and pain that existed in my life was necessary to help me to understand fully God's plan for my life. Our desire for relationship with Him must truly be a yearning for His companionship alone and not just His blessings. When I was young in the Lord and experiencing His goodness, I was not as occupied with my relationship with Him as I was tied to the blessings of knowing Him. We have to be careful of surrender to God that is motivated by what we can gain rather than intimacy with God Himself. Praise God for the journey.

Read Hebrews 12:5-11.

- What is God's goal in disciplining us?

Read 2 Corinthians 7: 9-10.

- What does Godly sorrow bring?

PRAYER TO EL ROI, THE GOD WHO SEES ME

I am poured out as a drink offering before You El Roi, My God Who Sees Me, and you sustain me in your strength and might through every battle. At times in my wandering and disobedience I have felt like throwing down the sword into the dust of this dry parched land and leaving it there. I have desired to just walk away and leave it for someone else to pursue. May I not despise your discipline, or resent your rebuke. You do this because you love me, as a father the one he delights in. Let me not completely forget this word of encouragement that addresses me as your child. May I not take lightly your hand of discipline or lose heart when You rebuke me, because You discipline those You love, and You chasten everyone You accept as Your child. May I always endure hardship as discipline; for it is in this that You remind me I am Your child. For what children are not disciplined by their father? May I always submit to the You, Father of the universe, and live! For I know You discipline me for my own good, that I may share in Your holiness. Though Your discipline does not seem pleasant at the time, but painful, I know it will produce a harvest of righteousness and peace in me as I am being trained by it. I now am happy, not because I was made sorry, but because my sorrow led me to repentance. For I became sorrowful as God intended, and so was led to Your heart. Godly sorrow has brought repentance that led to salvation and left no regret. So Lord, now take all the mistakes I have made along the way, as I wallowed in indecision and regret, and right the wrongs I may have caused in others' lives. For in that time I influenced others negatively, and I pray Your mercy and grace would redeem their lives as well. Your faithfulness remains. Your plan remains. Your love remains. Thank You Lord that I remain forever yours. In Jesus' Name I pray. Amen.

Chapter III

*But during the enemy's accusations of my unworthiness, You **Elohim Kedoshim, Holy God**, have called me to walk into a new land of your worthiness and I will not fall back; I will not give up.*

> *May God himself, the God of peace, sanctify you through and through. May your whole spirit, soul and body be kept blameless at the coming of our Lord Jesus Christ. The one who calls you is faithful, and he will do it (1 Thessalonians 5:23-24).*

Sometimes we think that by serving God with constant activity, we will attain a greater salvation. Jesus did all the work. Our service may be too much if we have no margins in our lives. If our relationships, health and rest are suffering, perhaps we need to seek a higher calling of sitting at the Savior's feet. Our unbroken communion and abiding with Jesus is our highest labor. In that, we will find that the abiding presence of God will result in our labor being His alone; all credit and all glory only God's.

Three-Dimensional Canvas

Puzzle pieces of our lives
Pictures shattered, scattered, worn
Dangling bits of energy
Scarred, consumed, and torn
Perfect landscapes shattered
Once meant for peaceful subsistence
Renewed only by Christ's touch
His care so sure, so ordered, and persistent
Breathing life and streams of grace
Into a two-dimensional life
Now a three-dimensional canvas

BITS AND PIECES

Our Abba Father canvasses the whole world 'in search' of one whose heart is interwoven with His. He handpicks each of us to accomplish remarkable tasks one moment at a time. Our lives are much like puzzles. We come into this world already broken in a thousand pieces it seems; trying to find an edge here or there to hang on to. We group our thoughts, our friends, our ideals, careers, family and possessions by like-colors, like-patterns, like-shades, like-shadows until we realize the different contrasts create greater beauty. We even group those out-lying pieces: people, disfigured pieces and misfits until we can find a proper place for them. But our Abba Father sees the completed picture. He knows the end from the beginning and He takes pleasure in the times we find "a fit" and start to see a portion of His plan. He rejoices over us with singing when the borders of our lives are set in place by the Word, His hand, His Spirit and His purpose. He celebrates the small victories when we start to see something we recognize as true. And once our journey here is complete, perhaps, like a puzzle finished, others will see the beauty of the picture of our lives, well-lived.

Many of us today live segmented lives, each puzzle piece angling to fit together to define who we are in this busy world. We have our families, our career, our hobbies, our fitness training, our friends, and sometimes, if we're blessed, our church. Each piece is worn at the edges as we try relentlessly to push them next to one another and find that they don't always fit. We leave few margins in our lives for nurturing our spirits that identify with a holy God. And if the pieces ever do fit together, it is for a fleeting moment. We struggle to see the completed picture of our lives from beginning to end, and many times it takes just one stressor for the picture to shatter. We stand, or many times fall to our knees, as we witness the scattered pieces before us and we ask "Why?" Those perfect landscapes we once dreamed for our lives lay scarred, consumed, and torn. This however, is not God's divine plan for our lives. When we align our will with His, then we can realize not only how much He loves us, but also His divine plan.

This defined a season of my life when my mind, heart, spirit, and soul were out of alignment with God's Truth and purpose for my life. I read a book by Henri Blackaby entitled "Experiencing God: Knowing and Doing the Will of God".[8] One truth he shared in that book was that when we do not see or understand which direction to take, we should draw near to what God is already doing. That one idea changed the trajectory of my life and hurled me into a supernatural walk with God that has become an amazing adventure. Look at what God is doing in your family, your church, and your community, and press into that as you continue to seek God with all your heart, mind, and will. Your alignment will come. He always leaves the choice in our hands; choose wisely!

The Word of God is a seed planted in us. Some of us have planted much in us, and some have little. Seeds are a miracle of life that I discover new each year, both naturally in my garden and supernaturally in my soul. Planting seeds in the natural can break apart rocks as they grow. Planting seeds in the supernatural can erode the hardness of our hearts and propel us into the divine call on our lives. The seed of the Word of God, planted in us, has the ability to grow into the parent plant. Created in God's image, men and women have the unique ability to realize right from wrong. We also have the unique ability to grow into our parent plant, the likeness and image of Jesus Christ. So whose DNA do you possess? Are you being nurtured in the Word of God and cultivated by His Spirit on a daily basis to grow into the image and likeness of Christ? Or are you being developed by this world and the lies of Satan to grow into his image and likeness; disfigured, torn, dying, and stolen. Those are our two choices. Either God the Father is your father, or Satan is your father. Eternity is real. Heaven and hell are real. This world will pass away, but the Word of God will last forever.

> *Then God said, "Let the land burst forth with every sort of grass and seed-bearing plant. And let there be trees that grow seed-bearing fruit. The seeds will then produce the kinds of plants and trees from which they came."* (Gen. 1:11).

> *Whosoever is born of God does not commit sin; for his seed remains in him, and he cannot sin, because he is born of God.* (1John 3:9)

This means we should not continually sin once we are born of the spirit and of God. Interestingly, the word 'seed' in Greek is the word sperma (sperm). As God plants the seed of His Word, which is Jesus Christ in your life, ought you not become more like Christ? Peter referred to this miraculous event when he wrote that, *"For you have been born again, not of perishable seed, but of imperishable, through the living and enduring the Word of God, which lives and abides forever"* (1 Peter 1:23). Once we are born of God, we carry the life and nature of God within us and He gives us a new nature. *"Therefore, if anyone is in Christ, the new creation has come: The old has gone, the new is here"* (2 Cor. 5:17).

May the Father of our souls consume us in His Spirit to be more like His Son, Jesus.

So how can we quiet the fears within us and approach not only a Holy God but a sinful world with hope? Ephesians 5:1 tells us, *"Follow God's example in everything you do, because you are his dear children."* This text tells us something about God's heart. It tells us that the character of God's heart is one of divine delight, divine permanency, and divine expression. We need to start displaying the characteristics of God for we are His representation on this earth. A father always longs for his own children to represent him well in the earth, and so too our heavenly Father. Jesus said, *"Very truly I tell you, whoever believes in me will do the works I have been doing, and they will do even greater things than these, because I am going to the Father"* (John 14:12).

We are His ambassadors on the earth and both Jesus and his apostles gave us examples to follow. Paul urged his followers to follow his own example in 1 Corinthians 4:16, *"Therefore, I urge you to imitate me."* This verse could be translated "I'm urging you to act like me! Watch what I do, and duplicate in your own life everything you see in me." Are you able to tell others to do that regarding your own life? Hebrews 13:7 uses the same idea when it states, *"Remember your leaders, who spoke the word of God to you. Consider the outcome of their way of life and imitate their faith."* This word 'follow or imitate' could be translated that you need to carefully model your faith after theirs: doing what they do, saying what they say, acting like they act and considering the great maturity and fruit produced by their lives. *"I have no greater joy than to hear that my children are walking in the truth"* (3 John 1:4). I have that Scripture near pictures of my children as it is my heart's prayer every day. Jesus said to follow him, not just believe.

When we do not have good mentors or leaders in our lives, we can sometimes get sidetracked for eternity. Let us compare how two women in the Bible approached their fears; one with a mentor and one without. The one in the Old Testament is Esther; the one in the New Testament is Drusilla. I'm sure you have heard of Esther, but I would wager Drusilla has not been on your radar much. Both were born of Jewish decent, both lost one or both parents at a young age, both were quite beautiful, both married pagan men, and both were confronted with truth in unique ways. It's their responses that differed greatly and ultimately affected their eternal destinies, and the destinies of countless others.

LESSON 3

QUIETING THE FEARS WITHIN

So, let's begin with Esther. This book in the Bible is ten chapters long. It's amazing that God's name is never mentioned in this text, but His actions are unmistakable. Esther and Mordecai risk their lives to save their people living in exile in Persia, just as Jesus came to rescue us as we live in exile here. This account, that led to the Jewish feast of Purim, is one in which timeless lessons are displayed for us. It would benefit you to do a relaxed read of this book at your leisure. The entire story is wonderful. For now though, we will focus on what may have caused Esther "fear" and what she chose to do about it.

Read Esther 1:10-22.

- Consider the time this took place. What amazed you regarding Vashti?

- What do you think motivated Vashti to act this way? Do you think fear entered in?

Read Esther 2:5-7.

- Why could Esther have 'chosen' to be bitter from youth?

Read Esther 4:12-17.

Esther models for us the importance of habitually following the advice and counsel of godly mentors and leaders.

- What are some habits in your own life? Have they resulted in good or bad results?

- Who in your life can you trust to be a godly mentor?

Read Esther 5:1-8:9.

Esther chose to put her life on the line and use her influence to help her people. We may not be asked in this life to make such a decision, but we are asked to conquer our fears and influence others.

- What fear did Esther have to face?

- How did she choose to approach this fear?

- How can we choose love over fear in our lives; with others and with God?

- Find some New Testament Scriptures regarding fear. What did you discover?

No one knows for sure why Esther petitioned the king for a second banquet, but perhaps she lost her nerve, or she discerned that the first banquet was not the right timing.

- Have you ever faced a situation where you felt the Holy Spirit speak to your heart, "Not now!"?

- Why might this "waiting pattern" be required sometimes when discerning the things of God?

- Consider Esther's example. What are we asked to do to gain godly wisdom in James 1:5-8?

- What fears do you face in your own life? How can you determine to use godly mentors and godly wisdom to combat your fears?

- To approach a Holy God we need to remember that He did make a new covenant of love through Jesus' death, burial, and resurrection. When we turn to Him, He receives us with open arms. He's actually the One who calls us to Himself. Have you experienced this amazing love? If so, when? If not, why not now?

DRUSILLA

Next, let's consider the life of our lesser-known woman, Drusilla. Her name is derived from Roman decent and means "watered by the dew". The record this woman left behind would have been quite different had she the courage of Esther. Unfortunately, she did not allow the dew of heaven to permeate her life or bring a change to those she knew. So, I know you are sitting there thinking, "Who is Drusilla anyway?" Look to the only Biblical account of her mentioned in Acts 24: 10-27.

Read Acts 24:10-27.

- Who was Drusilla?

- What is the only information offered here?

Though this is all we know of her recorded in Scripture, there is much information about her in other historical documents. She was related to some very famous individuals, which is why we know some other things about her. She was the granddaughter of Herod the Great, and the youngest of three daughters born to Herod Agrippa I. Herod Antipas, who beheaded John the Baptist, was her uncle. At fifteen, she married King Aziz of Emesa. King Aziz was circumcised to please Drusilla's father. Later, Drusilla was unfaithful to her husband. She illegitimately married Felix, the governor of Rome, while her first husband was still alive and no divorce had occurred. She bore Felix a son, named Agrippa. Drusilla was known for her great beauty, and her sister Bernice held great hatred for her. She was about twenty years old when she met Paul with Felix. Since Felix had once been a slave and then ended up a ruler of a Roman province, his personality was both brutal and treacherous. This caused both of them to tremble as Paul preached about his faith in Christ. Their own sins convicted them. Felix had wanted Paul to bribe him to let him go, but neither Felix nor Drusilla expected to hear what Paul had to say. They thought they would be entertained, but Paul spoke of righteousness, self-control, and judgement to come; they did not like that at all.

- What do you think you might have thought if Paul had been talking to you regarding righteousness, self-control, and judgement? How would you react if someone confronted known sin in your life?

Felix was convicted of abducting Drusilla, and Drusilla was convicted of being married to two men. Paul spoke to them with confidence and authority; he was not ashamed of the gospel he preached.

When the sword of God's Word cuts into our guilty sense of right and wrong, we have two choices: repent and be healed or run away from God and face eternal consequences. I am sorry to say it is believed that Drusilla ran. In the Scriptural text we know that Paul was sent back to prison as these two encountered the conviction of the Holy Spirit. Perhaps if Drusilla had not sat at Felix's side that day, he may have come to faith in Christ. Our relationships matter! Our counsel matters! Had this daughter of Abraham repented, who knows what grace would have rippled through the ages of time and peoples. Rather than kneel and repent, she chose to see Paul as her enemy and hated him for exposing her sin. That is exactly how some react to the gospel of truth. Sometimes, they react this way merely by our presence, for we carry the aroma of life and death.

> *But thanks be to God, who always leads us as captives in Christ's triumphal procession and uses us to spread the aroma of the knowledge of him everywhere. For we are to God the pleasing aroma of Christ among those who are being saved and those who are perishing. To the one we are an aroma that brings death; to the other, an aroma that brings life. And who is equal to such a task?* (2 Corinthians 2:14-16).

- Reflect on this text and record what the Holy Spirit speaks to your heart.

After Paul's trial, Felix and Drusilla disappear from our sacred text. Whatever became of these two who had the honor to listen to Paul preach in private sessions? Josephus, a historian who lived at about the same time, recorded that twenty years after Paul's transfer from Felix to Festus, Vesuvius erupted. When this happened, the affluent Pompeii and Herculaneum were buried under the burning lava. It is recorded that as many fled the catastrophe, Drusilla, seeking to escape with her child, Agrippa, was too late to elude disaster. She left the retreat too late with her son and both were buried beneath the lava. As she fell into the hands of the living God, only they two know her eternal state.

We have looked at two examples of women facing their fears. One chose godly counsel, prayer, and fasting. The other chose to remain in her own shame and hardened heart, to try to hide from a holy God and run away just as Eve did in the garden. The one showed courage and spiritual discipline. The other showed what happens when we idolize fleshly lusts over our Creator God's divine will and plan for our lives.

- I pray you identify with our example of Esther, but we have all chosen to run and hide at times because of fear if we are truly honest. If you could identify one thing in your life that you are running from facing today, what might it be?

- How do you believe God is calling you to react to this situation?

#3. The third obstacle that keeps us from enjoying a right relationship with the Father as His son or daughter, His prince or princess, is that we are not sure how to quiet the fears within us.

How to quiet the fears within us is through repentance and laying all our sins bare before a Holy God, Who already knows each one. Make no mistake, God is to be feared especially as we abide in complacency and apathy in our sin. He alone is holy. There is such a thing as a holy fear of a righteous God. However, as we are in relationship with God as His child, we can come to him without hesitation. As we humble ourselves completely honest before Him and repent, He wraps us in his loving arms. Today is the day of repentance and salvation. Today is the day to turn to Jesus Christ, for eternity will come to every man and woman. Will this be your experience when you pass from this earth?–*"I lie down and sleep; I wake again, because the LORD sustains me"* (Psalm 3:5).

When we find salvation and abide in Christ, we find rest for our souls. If you are anxious or distraught, come to Jesus and find rest. The Scriptures tell us in Psalm 46:2, *"Therefore we will not fear, though the earth give way and the mountains fall into the heart of the sea."* Yet, many of us live in desperate fear over all that is happening around us in the natural world.

"Do not call conspiracy everything this people calls a conspiracy; do not fear what they fear, and do not dread it" (Isa 8:12). In this current age who are we believing?

It all comes down to believing what the Word of God says or not. I choose to believe and I have peace. The Lord addresses people's fears in Malachi 3:5 when He says, *"So I will come to put you on trial. I will be quick to testify against sorcerers, adulterers and perjurers, against those who defraud laborers of their wages, who oppress the widows and the fatherless, and deprive the foreigners among you of justice, but do not fear me," says the LORD Almighty.* In other words fall into the hands of a holy God now in repentance or later in judgement; either way each of us will stand before Him. *"Everyone who does evil hates the light, and will not come into the light for fear that their deeds will be exposed."* (John 3:20). There it is, exposing our sin now brings salvation, peace, and rest for our souls; having them exposed by God after we die, will bring judgement and eternal death.

Many are living in bondage and slavery to the enemy of their souls and not counting the cost. They are listening to the lies of Satan that God is angry with them. Satan would like to take as many as possible with him into the lake of fire. Receiving Christ into our hearts and the Holy Spirit into our souls brings life and sonship. We are no longer slaves to the enemy of our souls as evidenced here: *"The Spirit you received does not make you slaves, so that you live in fear again; rather, the Spirit you received brought about your adoption to sonship. And by him we cry, "Abba, Father"* (Rom 8:15*).* If we are walking in fear, we are not walking in love because Scripture tells us, *"There is no fear in love. But perfect love drives out fear, because fear has to do with punishment. The one who fears is not made perfect in love"* (1John 4:18). We either, humble ourselves now before God and received His love, or we will be humbled by a Holy God at the judgement seat.

As you reflect, write and meditate on the following Scriptures, write down anything you are feeling or thinking:

Psalm 55:19

Proverbs 1:29

Proverbs 3:7

Jer. 5:22

Jeremiah 26:19–[You may want to read more of this portion of Scripture to get the context.]

PRAYER TO ELOHIM KEDOSHIM, MY HOLY GOD

Lord Elohim Kedoshim, my Holy God, You know how I sometimes want to throw down the sword into the dirt and walk on without it. When the enemy accuses me of my unworthiness I will remember Your name. I know you could raise up another, but You Elohim Kedoshim, Holy God, have called me to walk into a new land and I will not fall back; I will not give up. May You, God of peace, sanctify me through and through. May my whole spirit, soul and body be kept blameless at Your coming Lord Jesus Christ. You have called me and You are faithful. I know You will do it for You are the Author and Finisher of my faith. I am born of You Lord God and You empower me to not continue in my sin. You plant the seed of Your Word, Jesus Christ Himself, in my life, and I ought to become more like Him. Help me Lord. I have been born of incorruptible seed, by the Word of God, which lives and abides in me forever. You have given me newness of life and I now carry Your very nature. The old is gone, the new is come. You alone Lord have called me to such a time as this and I will not fall back. Give me courage Lord to face the trials and enemies of this life as I seek Your wisdom, Your counsel, and Your face. Grant me godly mentors in my life that will pray for me and keep me accountable. Grant me handmaidens to support me in the work You have called me to. May fasting and prayer be a discipline in my life to usher in your courage and holiness, replacing all fears. In Jesus' Name I pray. Amen.

BEGINNING TO LEARN WHO HE IS

Chapter IV

*When I have fear of rejection by others or even by You, You are the One **El Nekamoth, Who Avenges** me, sustains me, empowers me, and breathes new life into my being.*

> *"He is the God who avenges me, who puts the nations under me"* (2 Samuel 2:48).

My precious Dad died in February of 2002 from a very aggressive brain tumor. My three brothers and I were all at our parents' home with our families that Christmas of 2001. It was a blessed holiday, but Dad did not seem to be his usual jovial, cookie-eating self. He was quiet and was not talking much. None of us were sure why, but no one said anything at first. At one point the circuit breaker in the house tripped from too many lights, too many hair dryers, and too many people plugging things in. When my Mom asked Dad to take a look at the circuits, which were located in the basement, he walked into the living room and just stood there. He didn't seem to know where he was expected to go. At that point, we all got concerned. We also had gone to a movie and he was tripping a lot. Not wanting to upset our parents, we prayed individually and finished our holiday festivities before heading to our various homes.

That New Year's Day, I took my annual walk to contemplate the year ending and the new one beginning. As I was walking and praying, I remember asking the Lord for wisdom for the New Year. Just as I uttered the prayer, I saw a white owl. Its eyes mesmerized me, and I had the distinct feeling that truly wisdom would be imparted to me because the year ahead would have some challenges. Little did I know that those challenges would begin the moment I entered my house that day.

I called my parents to wish them a Happy New Year and my Dad answered the phone with "Hello".

I said, "Hi Dad, Happy New Year!" Now, you have to know that my Dad was a real kidder and he loved to tease me so at first I wasn't sure what was going on when silence followed.

He said, "What…?" then he said "Whoooo?" It was as though he could not retrieve the words.

I said, "Get Mom!"

There was a long silence until finally my Mom got on the phone. She said Dad was just sitting there holding the phone on his lap when she walked by. I told her to get him to the hospital, that I thought he may have had a stroke. Mom started to cry and admitted that she knew something was wrong for a while, but she didn't want to admit it to us or to herself. I called my brother John who lived close by and he called the ambulance. That began two months of hospital visits, the diagnosis of a ganglion brain tumor, and my traveling to Pittsburgh every other week from eastern Pennsylvania. I laid down my doctoral work and never felt the desire after that to finish. My employer was great at the time, and gave me family medical leave to help out at home. Dad died Feb. 26th that year and his death cut me in my spirit deeply. I had just been in Pittsburgh for a while and had driven home. I no sooner walked in the door when the phone rang; it was my brother telling me to come back, the hospice nurse said he probably only has a few hours. On my way back to Pittsburgh, about a five hour drive, a song came on the radio at 8:05 that included in its lyrics "I'm walking streets of gold." At that same moment I knew he had gone. When I got home, the medics were carrying him out in a black bag. My heart shifted, my spirit broke, and grief consumed me. He had died exactly at 8:05 PM.

You see, I had been ministering in the gift of healing at the time and I had seen the miraculous in many people's lives. Wrapping my spirit around the fact that God chose to heal others but take my Dad home to heaven was difficult for me. I know he received his ultimate healing and was with the Lord, but grief is still grief, even though I know I will see him again. I am not without hope. In this time, I began to write poetry again and for that I was blessed. I was beginning to understand the need to thank and praise God through the many storms. The following two poems were written in this season:

Pastel Hues

Pastel hues upon the ice
Reflect your glory Lord
Though wind and storm assail
May I never again be veiled

Patterns of such grace and glory
Silhouettes of death and life
Mingle to create such beauty
Even though amid such strife

I count your blessings Holy Lord
Both joy and sorrow, somehow crystallized
For without life's many contrasts
Your richness, perhaps, never realized

Lay your heart upon my own
Let me taste and see its richness
Let no fear ever govern me
For as we join, such sweetness

<u>This Place Called Grief</u>

This place called grief
So masked by pain
Tiredness unending
Yet your presence keeps me sane

I see you in the bleakest winter
Consolation in the pace
Your glory reflected on the ice
Pastel hues of grace

Your comfort is unending
Your heart upon my own
And I catch a glimmer
Our beings fully sown

You gave Your Son unselfishly
To bear my sin and shame
This weight upon your heart so great
Death holds no chains of blame

Because our Christ does live
Spring dawns and flowers
Upon our soul once more
The cycles of blessings' showers

Renew us day by day
As our hearts are joined as one
Create newness in my soul
Until we stand before your Son

Encounter Weekend Journal Entry–Sept. 16-18, 2005

Ezekiel 43:5 says, *"So the Spirit took me up, and brought me into the inner court, and behold, the glory of the Lord filled the house."*

Ezekiel 47 speaks of the river from the right side of the temple, the sanctuary and presence of God in Jerusalem. God has brought me through the waters of His Word and Spirit; to my ankles in my salvation, to my knees in prayer, to my waist in purity, until the waters covered me and I had to float in faith, and swim in evangelism. This river will flow from Jerusalem to the Dead Sea one day making it fresh and full of life. It will be a river of life flowing into the dead things of this world. The river of God's Spirit enters my spirit in greater measure as the years pass. In verse 47:9 we read, *"Swarms of living creatures will live wherever the river flows. There will be large numbers of fish, because this water flows there and makes the salt water fresh; so where the river flows everything will live."*

"There is a river whose streams make glad the city of God, the holy place where the Most High dwells" (Ps. 46:4).

"In that day the mountains will drip new wine, and the hills will flow with milk; all the ravines of Judah will run with water. A fountain will flow out of the LORD's house and will water the valley of acacias" (Joel 3:18).

"On that day living water will flow out from Jerusalem, half of it east to the Dead Sea and half of it west to the Mediterranean Sea, in summer and in winter" (Zech. 14:8).

A new time begins. Praise His precious name. What a weekend! God visited His people and moved powerfully once more in my life. Each session of the Encounter Weekend was just for me. In each one of the sessions, the Lord moved me one more degree closer to His heart and towards His face. He continued to separate the vinegar from the oil in my life; the dross from the gold. Praise God!

On Saturday, I had shared a morning devotional with the women in my room. It was on John 6 and how the apostles questioned Jesus about the body and blood He spoke of in the breaking of the bread. This was hard teaching for the apostles and they had a choice to accept and trust or turn away. Jesus asked them in John 6: 61, *"Does this offend you?"* We too are given those choices in the hard teachings Christ has for us. I asked the women to be ready for any hard teachings the Lord might have for them that day. Little did I know that He had one for me!

As we watched clips from the movie on the Passion, I was convinced that I could meditate on the Lord's suffering without viewing the awful violence of the visual presentation. As I closed my eyes, I heard the Lord impress on my spirit, "Open your eyes, this is the hard teaching I spoke of." I opened my eyes and tried to watch. I could not or would not and closed my eyes again. I prayed for it all to stop. I heard the Lord again, "Open your eyes, this is the hard teaching I spoke of." I tried to watch again and I could not. I closed my eyes and prayed to not have to watch my Lord suffer so. Again the Father said, "Open your eyes, this is the hard teaching I spoke of." Finally I watched it.

I noticed that everyone in the room was weeping except me. It startled me because I cry often over many things, and cry out to the Lord all the time. I asked the Father what was wrong and why could I not cry. All of a sudden, I felt such rage and anger that I could barely stay seated. It rose up in my spirit so suddenly I was not sure why. I asked the Father to help me discern my feelings. He said, "You've been angry at me too long. Be healed of this." I then could see and understand that I have been angry at the Father for a very long time. I could never understand why His will had to include the severe suffering of Christ. Though I understood and accepted salvation as a child, I was never positive of why Jesus had to suffer as he did. We had walked on our knees the Stations of the Cross since I was six; being "conformed" to Christ's suffering. I would cry over how great my Lord's suffering was, and why

He had called me to such suffering; which is how we were taught to identify with the suffering of Christ. Why could a loving Father require the beating and slaying of His Precious Son, His Precious Lamb, and my Precious Lord?

In the moment in the film when Christ gave up His spirit, my eyes were open to a severe truth in my life. As the Son of God willingly laid down His life for me in this sacrifice of love, mine was not to question why the Father required it, but to trust His authority in my life completely. My duty was to thank and worship Him for so great a gift of salvation. He fed into my spirit that my mind cannot conceive all the galaxies and universes He has created. He had used the night sky as part of my salvation experience, and was now showing me that my mortal mind could not conceive His will in all things. He asks me to simply trust Him and know His love is complete in the plan He has set forth from the old covenant of law in the Old Testament to the new covenant of grace in the New Testament. I understood this in other areas of my life, taught others this same truth, but in this hidden childhood anger my conscious mind could not comprehend without the Father's intervention.

As this truth settled in my heart, a new anger rose, and it startled me as much as the first. I then realized, I was angry at the Father for so many things: not understanding as a child why Jesus had to die such a terrible death, broken engagements, kidnapping and abuse, a broken marriage covenant, lost years of depression, and of course not being able to pray "enough" for the healing of my own father of his brain tumor a year and a half before. I have believed for others and the Father has been gracious, but for this one that I loved He seemed so distant in my requests. It was in the release of all these angers that the Father reminded me that every man's birth and death are known and determined by Him alone. I knew all these things in my mind from Scripture, but it took divine intervention to reveal truth past my confusions, pain, and anger in heart and spirit. I immediately repented and knew His perfect peace. At this point I wept. Understand this whole internal experience occurred as I continued to view the Passion of My Lord. At this exact moment Christ gave up His Spirit in the film, and as the Lord's eye gave up the Spirit and He ascended to the Father willingly, the Father's tear dropped. I was set aflame with the love the Father has for the Son and for me. He holds my tears and pain and knows my heart better than I know it myself. He showed me grace, and I freely wept in the freedom of His peace and love. He encircled me in His grace and pure joy filled me. He healed a wound in my heart, a childhood pain in my spirit, and a question in my subconscious mind that only He knew was even there. I Praise Him for loving me so.

Right after the above revelation, one of our pastors preached from the verses from Ezekiel that I opened this section with, and it confirmed to me how God longs for us to go deeper than we have ever gone before and enter into His River. He longs to fellowship with us and will not reject us. This was only one of the experiences I had on this encounter weekend. The Lord delivered me from accepting manipulation, which was a generational sin in my family. He allowed me to forgive one who violated me, know that vengeance is the Lord's, and He will avenge those who have come against me. He reaffirmed a vision for our church and fellowship that was confirmed by those gathered there concerning revival through small groups and close knit community. Needless to say God's transformational power worked miracles in my life that weekend, and I pray you are blessed to have read my testimony of His abiding, gracious, passionate, patient, all consuming LOVE.

"The LORD is a God who avenges. O God who avenges, shine forth. ... Unless the LORD had given me help, I would soon have dwelt in the silence of death. When I said, "My foot is slipping," your unfailing love, LORD, supported me. When anxiety was great within me, your consolation brought me joy" (Ps. 94:1, 17-19).

This is what the Lord says: *"Stand at the crossroads and look; ask for the ancient paths, ask where the good way is, and walk in it, and you will find rest for your souls"* (Jer. 6:16).

My God is the One who avenges us. He will bring justice to every situation that has transpired and will transpire in my life and yours. He is the great equalizer in this world of injustice. He came to conquer sin, death, and the grave. There is nothing that is hidden from Him, and we do not need to fear the one who will ultimately take vengeance on every evil in this world. He is the great equalizer in this world of sin and corruption. Oh, that we would all stand strong in the face of evil and not fear what man may do. Would that we would trust the God that dwells within us.

In Numbers 35:12-27 God provided cities of refuge for people accused of killing another. Israel had been a nomadic people and, to protect its community, had long relied on tribal law. These laws called for retaliation and revenge for any individual who had been killed to be avenged by another family member. When Israel began to settle down as a nation, it became necessary to live under civil law. As this new system was taking root many of those accused of manslaughter were killed before standing trial. God established these safe havens of refuge as temporary sanctuaries. He has in His nature to protect the innocent.

The idea of an avenger actually comes from this time where God established six cities in Israel where people could flee to ensure a fair trial or protection if they intentionally or accidentally killed someone. An avenger was someone chosen from the next of kin to avenge innocent blood; a life for a life. God protected those who fled to the safe cities from the avenger. If the death was proved to be an accident, the person could reside in the safe city until the high priest died, then they could return home and the avenger had no right to kill him.

Living in a democracy where individuals are considered innocent until proven guilty, this form of brutality may seem difficult to grasp. But in the first century church, this concept had historical roots in the culture of the Jewish people. Paul, in Romans 12:19-21 encouraged the new believers in Christ that God is their avenger when he wrote: *"Beloved, never avenge yourselves, but leave it to the wrath of God, for it is written, "Vengeance is mine, I will repay," says the Lord. To the contrary, "if your enemy is hungry, feed him; if he is thirsty, give him something to drink; for by so doing you will heap burning coals on his head." Do not be overcome by evil, but overcome evil with good."*

We are to turn our vengeance into the hands of Almighty God, and overcome evil with good. Let us not forget that our God is mighty and NOTHING is too hard for the Lord. He will avenge us.

We live in a fallen world under temporary dominion of an evil adversary that lies and steals and accuses us, and wants us to believe we are unworthy of God's love and grace. We confuse the God who will avenge us one day with a "vengeful God" who is out to get us. That is a LIE OF THE ENEMY to keep us from approaching God with a contrite heart of repentance.

God is the ultimate victor and He wants to reign in your heart and life, and give you victory over all the lies you have been fed over the years that you are not worthy of His mercy, grace, love, forgiveness, and peace. They are yours today as you repent of your sin, and ask Jesus to fill the void within you in this day of grace. Remember the verse Zephaniah 3:17, *"The LORD your God is with you, he is mighty to save. He will take great delight in you, he will quiet you with his love, He will rejoice over you with singing."* It is God's great love for us that quiets our fears. Psalm 36:7-9 agrees, *"How priceless is your unfailing love, O God! People take refuge in the shadow of your wings. They feast on the abundance of your house; you give them drink from your river of delights. For with you is the fountain of life; in your light we see light."* We must be careful to not confuse the avenging nature of God with complacency on our part. God still wants us to engage the culture, but to know that, ultimately, He will judge all those who harm us, betray us, reject us, or cancel us. Let us always keep those who have come against us in prayer; that their hearts will be softened and turn to the Living God. Jesus is the only religious leader of any religion who has an empty tomb, rose from the dead and is alive today!

In John chapter 4:27-42 Jesus had a discourse with a Samaritan woman and reached out to this supposed outcast of society in love, told her to repent of her sin, and drink from the wellspring of eternal life. He was compelled by the Holy Spirit to go to her; blessed are those who are not offended at Christ. Those taught of God truly desire to learn more. Our Savior, by teaching one poor woman, spread knowledge to a whole town. Each one of us matters to God; as does each person in our sphere of influence. As pebbles in a pond create concentric circles, so too our influence is far reaching either for good or for evil.

Isaiah 54:10 states, *"Though the mountains be shaken and the hills be removed, yet my unfailing love for you will not be shaken nor my covenant of peace be removed," says the LORD, who has compassion on you."* Remember, we come to God not in our own worthiness or righteousness, but in Christ's, whose righteousness the Father then sees us by, as through a lens filtering our sin by way of the blood of the cross. Just as God protected the people who fled to the cities from an avenger, He protects us as we hide in the cross of Christ. God protects His children still today from the accuser of the brethren, and one day will avenge all who have come against His children.

So how am I growing? God does not give up on His children. I am so thankful that when we take the time to be in His presence at His feet, He does some amazing things in our spirits. God comes into our lives to overcome the fears of rejection, confusion and abandonment. I know for me personally, I do not relish facing the hard things of life, because I am not always fully convinced of my Father's love for me when things seem to be going so wrong. I long to avenge myself. Yet there are so many examples in the Scriptures of how trials and suffering led to the great unfolding of God's love story with mankind. There are so many examples of His glorious unfolding of the story of my own life. I have a picture on my bathroom mirror that says, *"On the darkest days when I feel inadequate, unloved and unworthy, I remember whose daughter I am and straighten my crown!"* (Author unknown). I also remember that my Abba Daddy is my avenger, that I can place anything in his hand, and that He is faithful.

But what are you feeding on? Some of us shy away from God's presence because we fear He will reject us based on our past, our sins, or even our doubts. God is so much bigger than our finite minds can comprehend, and the new covenant of grace that Jesus came to bring us completes all that went before in the Law. Jesus is our sustenance. He is our bread of life. *"Jesus replied, "I am the bread of life. No one who comes to me will ever be hungry again. Those who believe in me will never thirst"* (John 6:35). Deuteronomy 8:3 tells us, *"Yes, he humbled you by letting you go hungry and then feeding you with manna, a food previously unknown to you and your ancestors. He did it to teach you that people need more than bread for their life; real life comes by feeding on every word of the LORD."* In Matthew 4:4 we read, *"But Jesus told him, "No! The Scriptures say, 'People need more than bread for their life; they must feed on every word of God."* And John 6:33 reads, *"The true bread of God is the one who comes down from heaven and gives life to the world."* Are you feeding on this bread of life, this Word of God?

LESSON 4

FEAR OF REJECTION

For it is not the one who commends himself who is approved, but the one whom the Lord commends (2 Corinthians 10:18).

Some of us have not really considered fear of rejection by God, because we are still caught up in our own fears of being rejected by men. We find approaching a holy God so far out of our comfort zone, when the lies of today have attracted our attention. When others do not acknowledge us, approve of us, or agree with us, we tend to feel rejected. We are so consumed with thoughts of self that we do not realize that others have not really considered our thoughts at all, or only have love toward us. Our own mind's battlefield is full of arrows thrown at a lot of people who have no clue what we are thinking or feeling. And the arrows fly towards us as well, but the instigator of those lies is not another person usually, but rather the enemy of our souls. *"We demolish arguments and every pretension that sets itself up against the knowledge of God, and we take captive every thought to make it obedient to Christ"* (2 Cor. 10:5). If we could only learn to take every thought captive according to the obedience of Christ, we would find more victory in our thought life. Some individuals do not feel rejected outwardly, but rather turn to boasting or pride to offset sub-conscience feelings of insecurity. Conviction of sin by a holy God can be misinterpreted as rejection.

Rejection is a learned feeling, and it can also be unlearned as we realize who we were always intended to be in Christ; how our Creator sees us and wants fellowship with us. Our approaching God does not depend on our own efforts. The God who created each one of us is the God who extends love to us in amazing ways, if we would but stop and look around. His Holy Spirit draws us to Himself. All of nature declares His glory, all the universes proclaim His praise. Your very body is so intricately and wonderfully created in His image as even your next breathe is held in His hand. He loved you so much that He sent His Son Jesus to die on a cross for you, to be the final sacrifice needed on this earth, and to fulfill the Law requiring a blood sacrifice for the sins of men. Wow! His love for you is so great.

So if we ever do consider God's acceptance, why is it that we usually feel rejection? Perhaps it is due to the fact that rejection is such a part of our human experience. Also, many of us have an Old Testament view of the Father that is in his law and judgement without His grace. On the other hand, some of us have a hyper grace-filled view that we forget His holiness and judgement altogether. Finding balance in His embrace is crucial. We are all spiritual refugees guilty of taking innocent blood, and we have fled the wrath of God to Jesus as our ultimate city of refuge. Jesus, our high priest, has died for us, and we have forgiveness with God. In Christ, great sinners receive God's protection from all of their enemies. And get this, the avenger now avenges us! Because God is our avenger, we do not have to be angry, insecure, bitter or vengeful any more. We can overcome evil with good, trusting that we do not have to win anymore; Christ is our Victor! God will usher in perfect justice for his people.

Read Joshua 20:1-9.
Define 'refuge'-

Read 2 Samuel 13:22 and 14:1-23.
Why were Jonathan and Saul the only two with swords according to I Sam.13:19?

Jonathan chose a rocky and unlikely route to attack the Philistines, yet God's favor was with him. Why do you think so?

Read Psalm 8:2.
What does this verse tell us about God's means to defeat our foes?

Reread Psalm 94:1, 17-19. What does it mean to you that God avenges you?

> *This is what the LORD says: "Stand at the crossroads and look; ask for the ancient paths, ask where the good way is, and walk in it, and you will find rest for your souls. But you said, 'We will not walk in it.' (Jer. 6:16)*

- Can you describe a crossroad in your life and did you make the right or wrong decision?

- What action can you take today to make a better choice regarding that?

Read Numbers 35:12-27.

> *Though the mountains be shaken and the hills be removed, yet my unfailing love for you will not be shaken nor my covenant of peace be removed," says the LORD, who has compassion on you (Isa. 54:10)*

- How is our Avenger also the one who has compassion on us?

#4. Another obstacle that keeps us from enjoying a right relationship with the Father as His son or daughter is fear of rejection by Him.

What has God promised us that allows us to come to Him without fear of rejection? In Jeremiah 32:38-41 we read, *"They will be my people, and I will be their God. I will give them singleness of heart and action, so that they will always fear me and that all will then go well for them and for their children after them. I will make an everlasting covenant with them: I will never stop doing good to them, and I will inspire them to fear me, so that they will never turn away from me. I will rejoice in doing them good and will assuredly plant them in this land with all my heart and soul."*

For years the people's hearts wandered from God. God pledges to focus their hearts on Him again. He vows to make them single-hearted, sincere, and consecrated in purpose. He will restore them to a love relationship with their Creator; realigning their purposes and desires toward God. Holy fear is a reverential awe of the majesty of God. He created each of us to fellowship with Himself with reverence. He realigns our purposes and desires just as He did for the people of the Old Testament, because our God does not change and His promises are true. His word is eternal and infallible. He will focus your heart on Him again. He vows to make you single-hearted, sincere, and consecrated in purpose. God your Father and Creator will restore you to a love relationship with Himself and realign your purposes and desires toward God. We recapture our innocence before God as His Word and Christ's blood wash us clean.

PRAYER TO EL NEKAMOTH, MY AVENGER

*When I have fear of rejection by others or even by you, you are the One **El Nekamoth, Who Avenges** me, sustains me, empowers me, and breathes new life into my being.*

You alone are the One who avenges me and puts the nations under me. You Lord are my refuge and strength. You have given me, like Jonathan, a spirit of courage and divine thought. Your wisdom is above the wisdom of man, and Your plans will prevail in the lives of men, as I trust in You alone. I will acknowledge that men are liars, but You alone God are true. You have established a stronghold against my enemies, and I will praise You all the day long. I will not trust in the weapons of man nor the schemes of this world, but I will trust in the Lord my God. Some trust in chariots and some in horses, but I will remember the Name of the Lord my God. I will sometimes be asked to take the steep and rocky path, but Your Spirit is ever upon me and will bring me victory. You will confirm your will to me through fellow soldiers in the battle and Your Holy Spirit, and nothing will hinder my God from saving me and those I love. So Lord, I ask today, avenge and obliterate injustice, intolerance, unforgiveness, bitterness, jealousies, greed, lust, lying spirits, Jezebel spirits, broken relationships, confusion, insecurities, wrong thinking, unrepentant hearts, disloyalty, and any other sin that may find root in our culture, my heart or in the heart of those I cherish. You alone are El Nekamoth, the One Who avenges me.

Chapter V

*In times of fears and doubts, You are the One **El Emunah, My Faithful God** Who calls me friend; Who calls me Your beloved, and walks within me, before me, behind me, and beside me.*

> *Know therefore that the LORD your God is God; He is the faithful God (El Emunah), keeping His covenant of love to a thousand generations of those who love Him and keep His commandments* (Deuteronomy 7:9).

Eternity Moved

Mary listened when the angel spoke
Eternity moved on the earth
Joseph listened to the dream as he awoke
Eternity moved on the earth
The Magi listened as they followed a star
Eternity moved on the earth
The shepherds listened to angels from afar
Eternity moved on the earth
Jesus listened to the Father's voice
Eternity moved every day on the earth
Modeling how to listen
Jesus moves on the earth
Adore Him and LISTEN.
Eternity moves through us.

Corners of My Heart

Corners of my thoughts
Release God's love to one
Become a garden of the Lord
Bedecked with God's own Son
A Bethany-Home for my Master
A place He brings His friends.
Needy ones to lay upon His breast
Corners of my thoughts and heart
Release God's love to one

Ever since the early 1980's, I had a desire to go to Romania and work with the orphans there. Our desires and prayers never go unanswered, they are merely on God's timetable. In 2009 I was blessed to go to Romania on a mission trip with my church. A woman, who I had met in my choir and also did prison ministry with, returned yearly to her homeland to minister. She is now a full time missionary in the country she escaped from in the early 1980's. The eight hour flight to Frankfort, four hour layover, two hour flight to Budapest Hungary, four and half hour bus ride to the border, one hour at the border, and then a seven hour bus ride to Ocan Mures, seemed to fly by because I was so excited to be going.

I had been struggling with a knee injury from my early 20's and in 2009 was wearing a metal knee brace, facing knee replacement surgery. I did not want to wear my brace on the plane, so I just took some pain medications along. It was a really long flight with layovers, and it took us over 26 hours to make the entire trip. When I got off the plane, my ankles were swollen and my knee was excruciatingly painful. I had to carry two large suitcases up a ramp; I could barely walk as it was. I prayed, "Father, you brought me on this trip, please heal my knee." I was tired and the exhaustion contributed to my urgency with the Lord. As I spoke the words, my knee clicked into place as though the brace, in the supernatural, had been set in place and I could walk. We had another miracle that same night as we climbed aboard a bus in the middle of nowhere to complete part of our trip and the engine would not start. We all prayed over the engine and it started. Praise God! I was not in any pain the entire time I was in Romania, and when I came home I continued to walk in my healing to this day; that was thirteen years ago. I am so grateful to the One who sees me.

The Lord also moved through all the team members in the gift of healing and spiritual warfare as we prayed for the people of Romania. We saw people delivered from demons, lives restored, and hundreds were set free from sin and disease in Jesus' Name. What a God we serve! The Lord was birthing new things in my spirit as I was learning the power of my resurrected Lord. I was beginning to understand how God longed for me to serve further in various ministries. Here are a few excerpts from my journal during that trip:

Aug. 1, 2009 – We went to a playground in Colonia in Ocna Mures for a medical outreach. I was on the prayer team and three couples gave their hearts and lives to the Lord. One couple was in their eighties, one in their mid-thirties, and one in their early twenties; three generations touched in one day. Praise God! May they impact their generations for you Lord. Many others prayed for salvation including several young boys, one named Anthony. In the afternoon there was a youth rally at the same playground, and the youth did a human video of the crucifixion. Many more came to Christ. Afterwards we prayed for more people. In the evening we ministered outside a church, because it was too hot inside the building. Praise You Lord for all You are doing!

Monday, Aug. 3, 2009 -Praise You Lord! Ministering in Romania is incredible. Today we went to a gypsy village (Silivasi) and the memory of the sights and sounds there will forever be etched in my memory. The stark poverty, filth, and depravity were unlike anything I have ever experienced personally in my life. There were naked babies with dogs on ropes, 13 year old mothers, mud huts with TV dishes on top, and men in high topped hats leaning against their makeshift hovels. I met a young man named Micah from the Peace Corps. We had a medical clinic, children's outreach, and a small service. Many came to Christ. I will never forget the woman who stood on the hill above us with arms outstretched in prayer as she prayed for her people during the entire service. A missionary named Caprise was so sweet with the people; she had the sweet fragrance of Christ as she loved on these overlooked ones. May I never forget the world's forgotten ones.

My roommate struggles with severe depression and anxiety and I pray you are using me in her life. Given the long trip, two hours of sleep, a full day of ministry and now several days with little or no sleep due to ministering to her, I'm exhausted. She goes home tomorrow because of the struggles she is having here. Ministering to her at night leaves me little time for rest but you are so faithful in strengthening me Lord. Help her to find peace Lord.

Tuesday, Aug. 4, 2009 – We went to Veresmont, Surgio and Lilly's (missionaries) village and orphanage for the day. We prayed near a very busy road with cars speeding by and God remained faithful. A middle-aged man named Chubby rededicated his life to the Lord. An older man named Paul sat on the fence of decision, but sadly turned away. An older man named Anton came for healing from pain in his legs from a Communist van that ran him over when he was young. We went to the orphanage for lunch, and prayed for three young boys who were hungry for more of God. They were baptized in the Holy Spirit. We had an evening service where many came to the Lord. The harvest was so ripe, the missionaries so humble and faithful, the Presence of God so sweet. We also had an evening service at Niko and Caprice's Good Samaritan Church, and had tea for the women there.

Wednesday, Aug. 5, 2009 – Praise God! We traveled to Santa Marie today and three people are in my room right now trying to fix the air conditioner. When we got to Ocna Mures we had no water the first night so I guess no air is not that bad. Praise God! The ride here was beautiful. The hillsides are covered with sunflowers, red roofs, sheep and shepherds, horses, carts, and meandering roads filled the vista. The faces of the people will long be remembered. We even had the blessing of a rain shower and rainbow. I feel I have not had time to sufficiently journal all the blessings of this time. The village we ministered to yesterday was very special. We did a medical prayer outreach in the morning and early afternoon; many gave their heart to Jesus. Some came and said they had no medical needs but wanted "to come to receive your Jesus, the God you serve." The people were so hungry for God.

Thursday, Aug. 6, 2009 – A morning of needed rest, we started ministry at 3:00. I gave my testimony at a small village church in Santa Marie. It was a very traditional Pentecostal church with overtones of Catholicism or Orthodox. Many came to salvation. I am undone.

Friday, Aug. 7, 2009 – Ministered at Ana's village in Micula Noua and another one that was very traditional in the Orthodox sense. We had a tea for the women in the afternoon and played games with the children. There were many blond children here, Swedish looking. We were told that the village was a Hungarian village since it was so close to the border. Many of the children came to church holding hands, two by two. They genuflected and prayed at the back of the church. After Greg prayed over the people, he asked me to share my testimony during the service and give the salvation prayer- what an honor to lead them in prayer! Once again, many gave their hearts to Christ. I will never forget that bright blue church, silhouetted against a beautiful sunset as children played in the yard, in the middle of nowhere, and these beautiful people raised their voices in worship.

Saturday, Aug. 8, 2009 – Today I taught a lesson at the Women's Tea outreach in Ana's village. I woke and the Lord gave me this passage- Isa. 53:11, *"by His knowledge my righteous servant will justify many, and He will bear their iniquities."* I shared a testimony of Christ's righteousness and how He alone can bear our iniquities. I pray you were honored Lord through me; may Your praise and glory ever be on my lips. One woman today was delivered from demons; what a witness of the power of our God!

Sunday, Aug. 9, 2009 – We ended our time in Romania with a Sunday service at Ana's church and lunch at her brother's house. Then we took a seven hour bus ride to Budapest near the airport. I am staying an extra day with a few others to tour Budapest. (That didn't happen as I got very ill and stayed in bed until I could return home.)

LESSON 5 A

Laying Aside Doubt
Running with Faith

As I have ministered to many women over the years at church, in the prisons, in Bible studies, and even in Romania, two things seem to hold them in bondage above all else. One is fear and the other doubt. I admit I have struggled with both these demons in my own life. I tell people often that there is linear continuum between God and His unfathomable love and the enemy's hatred and lies. Fear and doubt as we tend to experience them in the natural are on the end of the enemy's spectrum. Fear and reverence for God at the other end of that eternal spectrum. As we begin this lesson, review the following Scriptures concerning doubt, as written, and then within the context of their chapters. Then answer the questions below.

And thy life shall hang in doubt before thee; and thou shalt fear day and night, and shalt have none assurance of thy life (Deut. 28:66).

You of little faith," he said, "why did you doubt? (Matt. 14:31).

Jesus replied, "I tell you the truth, if you have faith and do not doubt, not only can you do what was done to the fig tree, but also you can say to this mountain, 'Go, throw yourself into the sea,' and it will be done (Matt. 21:21).

When they saw him, they worshiped him; but some doubted (Matt. 28:17).

I tell you the truth, if anyone says to this mountain, 'Go, throw yourself into the sea,' and does not doubt in his heart but believes that what he says will happen, it will be done for him (Mark 11:23).

He said to them, "Why are you troubled, and why do doubts rise in your minds? (Luke 24:38).

Then he said to Thomas, "Put your finger here; see my hands. Reach out your hand and put it into my side. Stop doubting and believe" (John 20:27).

But when he asks, he must believe and not doubt, because he who doubts is like a wave of the sea, blown and tossed by the wind (James 1:6).

Be merciful to those who doubt (Jude 1:22).

- How would you define doubt?

- What do these Scriptures indicate is the opposite of doubt?

- What would you say are your current doubts?

- Can you find a Scripture promise/reference opposite your doubt?

Don't Let Doubt Determine Your Destiny

Have you ever wished you could actually see Jesus, touch him, and hear his words? Are there times you want to sit down with Him and get His honest advice? Thomas wanted Jesus' physical presence and proof of His resurrection in the passage we will read here. But God's plan is wiser. God has not limited Himself to one physical body, He wants to be present with each individual at all times through His Holy Spirit. He wants to be so present with each of us that we can hear His voice through the pages of His Word. You can talk to Abba Father, and you can find God in the pages of the Bible. He can be as real to you as Jesus was to Thomas. If you have doubts today about who Jesus is, or whether or not He was resurrected, perhaps you, like Thomas, can declare, "My Lord and My God!" Jesus longs to reveal Himself to you through the Word. A great resource for those who doubt is *Evidence That Demands a Verdict: Life Changing Truth for a Skeptical World* by Josh and Sean McDowell.[9]

Thomas' story might sound a bit like your own when it comes to believing that Jesus rose from the dead. Read that portion of Scripture in John 20:19-30. Thomas' story is really many of our own. He doubted Jesus was the resurrected Christ, but his doubting had a purpose; he wanted to know the Truth! Have you ever struggled with this question, or with doubt over whether or not God is truly with us? The doubt of who Jesus is and why He came? Better to doubt out loud than to disbelieve in silence. It is pretty ironic that we never seem to doubt our physical world. We trust the laws of physics to be constant:

- Wooden solid chair- I sit on it with hardly a thought of its ability to hold me.
- Liquid water quenches my thirst- I rarely doubt it will.
- Breathe in oxygen involuntarily- I don't even consider it unless I have a problem.

As we have grown in a physical environment, we learn that solids are hard, liquids flow, and gases exist, but for many of us we have not grown up in a spiritual environment. Our spirits are starving in doubt, because we have not experienced spiritual truths, or had models to display God's glory in our lives. But the Word tells us, in Psalm 19:1-4:

"The heavens declare the glory of God; the skies proclaim the work of his hands. Day after day they pour forth speech; night after night they reveal knowledge. They have no speech, they use no words; no sound is heard from them. Yet their voice goes out into all the earth, their words to the ends of the world." God uses many means to reach His people so we are without excuse. He found me without a preacher or an evangelist. He found me by his Holy Spirit.

Study these Scriptures as to how God reaches people:

He uses His Creation (Ps. 19:1-4)
He uses Our Conscience (Romans 15:2)
He uses Natural Comforts (John 16:5-15)
He uses Conviction of Sin (John 16:5-15)
He uses Conversation around us (Romans 10:8-10)

We need only to listen and be still and know that He is God. We need to learn about the spiritual realm to be better equipped to operate there. His Word and His Spirit provide all we need. *"The Word of God is living and active, sharper than any double-edged sword, it penetrates even to dividing soul and spirit, joints and marrow, it judges the thoughts and attitudes of the heart"* (Heb. 4:12). In our main passage from John 20 we see that Jesus had witnesses to His resurrected body: here were the 10 disciples but others had seen Jesus too. There were the two men on road, the crowd of five hundred, Jesus' brother James, Mary Magdalene, Peter in Jerusalem; all testifying that Jesus had risen. These were eye-witnesses of Jesus' resurrection; physical evidence!

The truth of Christianity hinges on Christ's resurrection. Who saw him and were they reliable? They gave their lives for this cause; I would have to doubt that they did not see Jesus after His death. People rarely die for a cause if they were not sure it is true. These individuals turned the world upside down.

Jesus came to restore us. When He spoke to the Samaritan woman, Jesus answered her, *"If you knew the gift of God and who it is that asks you for a drink, you would have asked him and he would have given you living water"* (John 4:10). In Psalm 22:14 we learn, He was *'poured out like water'* and just as water poured from His side, Thomas wanted to place his hand in Jesus' side. I pray we have learned that God Himself has breathed the breadth of life into each one of us (Gen. 2:7), and he comes into our lives afresh to breathe on us the breadth of His Holy Spirit (John 20:22). We have eternal spiritual life with the power to do God's will on the earth. We are called to spread His Good News of salvation if we have settled the issue of our own salvation through repentance. These are Spiritual truths we can enter eternity with!

Like Thomas we tend to not think we are so bad really. What we know about Thomas actually sounds a lot like us...

- Likely a fisherman – good trade/ John 21:2
- Follower of Jesus – others saw this/ Luke 6:13-16
- An Apostle –a friend of Jesus/ Luke 6:13-16
- Loyal and Committed/ John 11:16.
- Confused sometimes / John 14:5

Your thoughts determine your reality, Jesus identified with the Father and said it was by His authority that He did the works He did. He passed on the job of spreading the good news of salvation around the world to His followers. Whatever God asks us to do remember that your authority comes from God, and Jesus is the One who demonstrated by words and actions how to accomplish the job He has given us. Confusion is the enemy's weapon, not God's. Be sure of who you identify with! Your thoughts must rule your emotions, not the other way around. *"We demolish arguments and every pretension that sets itself up against the knowledge of God, and we take captive every thought to make it obedient to Christ"* (2 Cor. 10:5)

Feelings make terrible masters and are terrible indicators of Truth. Our intellect must precede our emotions. Paul Valery, a French poet, essayist and philosopher of the mid 1800's said, "Our most important thoughts are those which contradict emotions."[10]

Thomas doubted Jesus' resurrection because he didn't see with his eyes, and Jesus told him in John 20:29, *"Because you have seen me you have believed; blessed are those who have not seen me yet believe."* And 1 Corinthians 2:9 reminds us, *"However, as it is written: "What no eye has seen, what no ear has heard, and what no human mind has conceived"— the things God has prepared for those who love him."*

Thomas doubted: he wanted to put his finger in Jesus' hands and his hand in Jesus' side. Jesus' hands that were stretched out on the cross, casting our sins as far as the east is from the west. Jesus' side was pierced and the water and blood poured out for our salvation; the perfect Lamb sacrificed for us. I wonder why Thomas did not ask about the crown of thorns, encircling Jesus' mind; the same mind that is steadfast and faithful and interceding for us to know Him, trust Him, and come to Him. Thomas did not ask about Jesus' feet that were pierced for our transgressions, shod with the gospel of peace. The enemy came to steal, kill, and destroy Jesus, but not even the grave could hold our Savior back.

Jesus was not hard on Thomas for his doubts. He was patient and kind. Despite his skepticism, Thomas was still loyal to the believers and to Jesus through it all. Some people need to doubt before they believe. Doubt is not a bad thing if we are truly searching for truth. If doubt leads to questions, and questions lead to answers, and truth is accepted, then doubt has done a good work. It is when doubt becomes stubbornness and leads to prideful lifestyles that doubt harms our faith. When you doubt, do not stop there. Let doubt deepen your faith as you continue to search for answers.

Our thoughts are our responsibility. We can use turn-around Scriptures to negate our negative thinking.

- *"Set your minds on things above, not on earthly things"* (Col. 3:2).
- *"We demolish arguments and every pretension that sets itself up against the knowledge of God, and we take captive every thought to make it obedient to Christ"* (2 Cor. 10:5).
- *"Finally, brothers and sisters, whatever is true, whatever is noble, whatever is right, whatever is pure, whatever is lovely, whatever is admirable—if anything is excellent or praiseworthy—think about such things"* (Phil. 4:8).
- *"You will keep in perfect peace those whose minds are steadfast because they trust in you"* (Isa. 26:3).
- *"Submit yourselves, then, to God. Resist the devil, and he will flee from you"* (James 4:7).

John 20:19-26 is our main text.

Our doubt can send us into a downward spiral, because the voice we believe will determine the future we experience. Satan sometimes uses our past to manipulate us in our insecurities to influence our destiny. We all have insecurities, but God's Word can develop our identity and overcome those insecurities. His Spirit can strengthen our resolve to walk in Kingdom power. Remember Ephesians 2:10, *"For we are God's handiwork, created in Christ Jesus to do good works, which God prepared in advance for us to do."* When we accept Christ, we take His Name. We have his Holy Spirit in us so whatever He is, we are!

We can move beyond doubt by making powerful declarations.

In John 20:28-29, *"Thomas said to him, "My Lord and my God!" Then Jesus told him, "Because you have seen me, you have believed; blessed are those who have not seen and yet have believed."* Can you draw in this spiritual truth and apply it to your own life without physically seeing Jesus? Do your spiritual eyes see this and does it give you a hunger for His Word? *"He was wounded for our transgressions. He was bruised for our iniquities; the chastisement for our peace was upon Him and by His stripes we are healed"* (Isa. 53:5). Are we able to get to the place Thomas finally did in vs. 28 when he said, *"My Lord and My God"*? I pray so, for your eternal destiny is at stake. Go from doubt to your divine destiny today.

LESSON 5 B

Laying Aside Fear
Running with Trust

Review the following Scriptures concerning fear, as written, and then within the context of their chapters. Then answer the questions below.

> *"Say to those with fearful hearts, "Be strong, do not fear; your God will come, he will come with vengeance; with divine retribution he will come to save you"* (Isa. 35:4).

> *"Peace I leave with you; my peace I give you. I do not give to you as the world gives. Do not let your hearts be troubled and do not be afraid"* (John 14:27).

> *"Have I not commanded you? Be strong and courageous. Do not be afraid; do not be discouraged, for the LORD your God will be with you wherever you go"* (Josh. 1:9).

> *"Therefore do not worry about tomorrow, for tomorrow will worry about itself. Each day has enough trouble of its own"* (Matt.6:34).

> *"But now, this is what the LORD says—he who created you, Jacob, he who formed you, Israel: "Do not fear, for I have redeemed you; I have summoned you by name; you are mine"* (Isa. 43:1).

"Even though I walk through the darkest valley, I will fear no evil, for you are with me; your rod and your staff, they comfort me" (Ps. 23:4).

"I sought the LORD, and he answered me; he delivered me from all my fears" (Ps. 34:4),

"When anxiety was great within me, your consolation brought me joy" (Ps. 94:19).

"The LORD is my light and my salvation—whom shall I fear? The LORD is the stronghold of my life—of whom shall I be afraid?" (Ps.27:1)

- How would you define fear?

- What do these Scriptures indicate is the opposite of fear?

- What would you say are your current fears?

- Can you find a Scripture promise/reference opposite your fear?

Lord willing, as you studied the above Scriptures, you found that faith and trust are the opposites of the two most debilitating emotions in our world- fear and doubt. The struggle we have as Christians is that as long as we walk outside our identity in the Kingdom, these two demons of our heart, mind, and soul will plague us as if we were pincushions for the enemy's pleasure. So how can we get victory over them? Begin by knowing that Satan always questions our identity. He even questioned Christ's. John the Baptist baptized Jesus and the Holy Spirit descended upon Him like a dove. God the Father spoke and told everyone standing there that this was his son and He was pleased with Him. Immediately thereafter, Jesus is led into the desert to be tempted by the devil. Satan says "If you are the son of God". He is questioning Jesus identity. When the enemy of our soul questions our identity, it opens a door to doubt and fear in our lives. Just like Jesus, we must guard against that happening. That's why Proverbs 4:23 says, *"Above all else, guard your heart for everything you do flows from it."* What is flowing from our hearts and impacting our spouse, our family, our neighborhood, our community, our nation? This is important, not just for your benefit, but for all those around you. You may not think your fears and doubts impact anyone but you, but on the contrary, they destroy lives. I know because I lived with fear for a long time, and it impacted my family greatly. To stop generational sin, to turn the tide of bloodline addictions, to stem the flood of the enemy's influence in our emotions, we need to get this right. Let us consider Joshua's story.

Read Deuteronomy 31:1-8. God had told Joshua to be strong and courageous; to not be terrified for God had given him the land. When God says something is ours, let us not fail to obey Him in going after it. God appropriated His authority to Joshua, but Joshua still had to receive it, and then walk in it. Walking in our God-given authority and identity manifests God's perfect will on the earth and in our lives. When we have a revelation of who Jesus is, and then walk in that revelation, demons listen and flee. Consider the story in Mark 9 and Luke 9 of the man who was driving out demons in Jesus' Name; the disciples wanted him to stop. Jesus told them not to stop him. This was before Jesus was crucified, before He rose again, and before Pentecost. Jesus' name holds authority and Holy Spirit moves as He will.

Healing is the same way. To heal from fear or doubt we need to get up and do something. That something is planting our faith anchor deep in the recesses of Christ's Truth, so that it becomes a firm foundation that will never be shaken. We do that by appropriating the Word of God in our spirit and being baptized in the Holy Spirit. The Lord healed me by keeping my focus outward on Him and others, not inward on myself. If the enemy of our soul can keep us inwardly focused, he will steal our dreams and our destiny. If we are not relying on the Holy Spirit and in the Word daily this is impossible. We cannot rely on Sunday sermons to feed us all week. We must be feeding on the Word of God daily and listening to the Father's voice through worship and prayer.

Who is your favorite person in the Old Testament? Mine is Elijah; ok, at least he is one of them. Read about his story in 1 Kings 17-21 and 2 Kings 1-3 and 9-10. He commanded the skies to hold back rain and they did (1 Kings 17:1; James 5:17-18). He was fed by ravens. He called down fire from Heaven and killed the prophets of Baal and Asherah on Mt Carmel. He also called down fire from Heaven on King Ahab's soldiers twice. He raised the widow's son from the dead (1 Kings 17:33). He parted the Jordan River. He did not do that by living in fear or doubt, but by the Spirit of the Living God! He was a man, flesh and blood, just like us. He was anointed for a purpose. The Holy Spirit anoints each of us as we continue to yield to His voice.

Jesus gives us His authority as His church and bride. *"I will build my church, and the gates of hell shall not prevail against it. I will give you the keys of the kingdom of heaven, and whatever you bind on earth shall be bound in heaven, and whatever you loose on earth shall be loosed in heaven"* (Matthew 16:18-19).

I totally misunderstood this. I thought God calls us into a strong tower, protecting us. Of course, that can be our first awareness of faith, because we have been so beat up by the world. Eventually however, we need to become offensive in the battle as we mature in faith. However, we dare not engage in that battle unprepared, unequipped, or unregenerated by a Holy God and His Word. We are to bow in holy reverence before the Judge of all creation daily, and then stand boldly in the face of the enemy and his lies. We are to repent of all known and unknown sin in ourselves and in our blood-line,[11] Jesus, our Advocate, then frees us from the enemy's accusations, and we are brought into divine alignment with our Father. Once free from those accusations, we can begin to partner with the Holy Spirit in tearing down the gates of hell and setting the captives free; free from sin, sickness, poverty, and addictions. Jesus gave us the keys to the kingdom: binding and loosing, sowing and reaping, proclaiming and declaring. *Jesus said "He who believes in me will do even greater things"* (John 14:12). We have Power of Attorney to heal and deliver in Jesus name.

"And these signs shall follow them that believe; In My name shall they cast out devils; they shall speak with new tongues: They shall take up serpents; and if they drink any deadly thing, it shall not hurt them; they shall lay hands on the sick, and they shall recover" (Mark 16:14-18).

The kingdom of heaven suffers violence and the violent take it by force; not physical violence, but spiritual violence. Violence in intercessory prayer on our knees; a travail of our spirit before God to push back the gates of hell. The kingdom is within each of us. We are not just divine vessels, but the very holy of holies of His presence. Christ in you is truly the hope of glory.

All of creation groans for the children of the King to recognize their inheritance in His Kingdom. God's desire is for us to walk in faith not doubt, to walk in trust not fear. We must choose holiness over anything else, laying down every idol, laying down every fear, laying down every doubt.

#5. Two other obstacles that keeps us from enjoying a right relationship with the Father as His son or daughter are doubt and fear. Whatever we are doubting is because we are not trusting the Word of God, we are not trusting Jesus Himself. For every doubt has a corresponding word from Scripture to declare and decree over the doubt. We might doubt He placed us on the right path but we must declare

Psalm 119:133, *"Order my steps in your word: and let not any iniquity have dominion over me."* We might doubt our daily assignment but we must declare Luke 10:2. And then ask, "Is it me Lord?" We may doubt if we have enough effort for the task at hand, but we must declare 2 Peter 3:14 and personalize it. He supplies all my needs. He is my strength and song. We may doubt our own abilities and wisdom, but then declare Proverbs 4:11. We may doubt that God will remove all the thorns from our life, but then declare Psalm 57:2. We may doubt that God has truly taken away our stain of sin, but then we must remember and decree Revelation 1:5. We may doubt our standing before a holy God, and then must decree I John 1:7. We may doubt God's process, but declare Isaiah 61:11. When we doubt and fear the things we see with our eyes and experience in our lives, God is calling us into a higher realm of his love, his glory, and his invisible kingdom. He is calling us to have greater faith in believing, and greater trust in His love. I believe that is why we too need to cry out, "Lord, give us greater faith." As the Lord leads us from faith to faith, from glory to glory, He is moving us forward in forming Christ in us. Rather than fighting this molding on the potter's wheel, yield to what challenges this chapter may have confronted you with. Let us truly discipline ourselves to pursue more of what true faith and trust entail. If you are not satisfied with where you currently are spiritually, keep seeking the face of God and He will reveal to you how much He loves you. It is in the revelation of His love that we find peace, in His presence that we find wholeness, and in His Spirit that we find direction for our lives. Pray the following prayer over yourself to declare and decree these things over your life.

Prayer to El Emunah, My Faithful God

El Emunah, My Faithful God, from the rising of the sun to the setting of the same, You have been so faithful to me. You surround me in protection, guide me in paths of righteousness, and walk beside me in rest or in toil. Even in times when I did not feel or acknowledge You,

You have protected and guided me. Your voice Lord is all I long to hear, and Your ways are my delight. I yearn to be faithful to You and others Lord, as You have always been faithful to me. I stand on your promises Lord to negate all doubts in my heart, mind or spirit. I pray for the hidden manna of heavenly mysteries. When I am doubting or fearing, help me to trust the Word of God, and You Jesus. I know now that every doubt or fear has a corresponding word to declare and decree over it, and I will search your Word as for hidden treasure Lord. When I doubt you have placed me on the right path, I will declare Psalm 119:133, *"Order my steps in your word: and let not any iniquity have dominion over me."* When I doubt or fear my daily assignment I will declare Luke 10:2 where You Jesus told them, *"The harvest is plentiful, but the workers are few. I will ask the Lord of the harvest to send out workers into his harvest field and then ask, "Is it me Lord?"* When I doubt if I have enough effort for the task at hand, I will declare 2 Peter 3:14 and personalize it, *"I will make every effort to be found spotless, blameless and at peace with him."* You Lord supply all my needs. You are my strength and song. I may doubt or fear my own abilities and wisdom, but then I will declare Proverbs 4:11, *"that you will instruct me in the way of wisdom and lead me along straight paths."* You alone Lord will teach me wisdom's ways and lead me in straight paths. I may doubt or even fear that God is showing me hidden things, but then I will declare Deuteronomy 29:29, *"The secret things belong to the Lord our God, but the things revealed belong to us and to our children forever that we may follow all the words of this law."* I may fear or doubt that God will show us the mysteries of His Kingdom, but then declare Isaiah 45:3, *"He will give me hidden treasures, riches stored in secret places, so that I may know that He is the LORD, the God of Israel, who summons me by name."* I may doubt that God will remove all the thorns from my life, but then declare Psalm 57:2, *"I will cry out to God Most High, to God who performs all things for me."* I may doubt that God has truly taken away my stain, but then I must remember and decree Revelation 1:5, *"And from Jesus Christ, who is the faithful witness, the first begotten of the dead, and the ruler of the kings of the earth ... who hath loved us, and washed us from our sins in his own blood".* I may fear or doubt my standing before a holy God, and then I must decree I John 1:7, *"But if we walk in the light, as he is in the light, we have fellowship one with another, and the blood of Jesus Christ his Son cleanses us from all sin".* I may doubt God's process but declare Isaiah 61:11, *"For as the soil makes the sprout come up and a garden causes seeds to grow, so the Sovereign LORD will make righteousness and praise spring up before us all."* I declare that you Lord have taken fear and doubt from my heart and delivered me into my calling and my destiny. I will not fear what man can do to me even unto death. I will be formed in your image Lord, and learn from the examples of your prophets, disciples, and saints. I yearn for the treasures of your kingdom and know that as I seek You, You are ever faithful to meet me here. May your character El Emunah be formed in me as a faithful servant with greater faith and trust than ever before. Amen.

Chapter VI

*You are **Adonai, Master over All**, the One who wears the Victor's Crown and I pledge my undying devotion to You. You have called me out of any mixture with this world. You call me anew and afresh to come and receive a new sword from You. You have more for me and so I come; to be restored, equipped anew, to go out yet again and face the giants. This time though, I go out in greater power, in greater anointing and in greater strength than ever before for You, Immanuel, are ever with me.*

"Oh Lord God, You have begun to show Your servant Your greatness and Your mighty hand, for what god is there in heaven or on earth who can do anything like Your works and Your mighty deeds" (Deut. 3:24).

Scepter, Signet, Sword

His scepter is held out to me
He says, "My child come"
I kneel in worship at His feet
He says, "Rise up, stand strong"

His signet ring is held out to me
He says, "My authority is yours"
I gaze in awe at this gift He brings
He says, "Rise up, do the work"

His sword is held out to me
He says, "My Princess wield it well"
I gaze into the depths of it
He says, "Rise up, the battle's won"

Journal Entry May 9, 2009

Praise You Lord! Thank You for using this vessel and giving me visual evidence of Your love. I was at the prison for one-on-ones and met with a young woman who I had been seeing for about eight months. She was being released on Friday. We talked about how God had transformed her life. I looked at her ID badge and the picture that stared back at me was not even the same woman that sat before me. When she entered prison months earlier, her very countenance was dead. She had lifeless eyes, her skin was pale and sallow, and her soul screamed out from a frightening countenance. The young woman of 20 years that sat before me today was not the same woman. Her eyes were bright and shining, her color robust and full of life, her countenance one of joy and optimism. Only my God can transform a life like that! We do not always see it in the months and years of our own life, but boy was I able to see it in hers over just a few months. And this is just one of the many lives

I have witnessed changed before my very eyes. Thank you Lord for the privilege of having a front row seat to your miracle working power, your saving grace, your great love for the hurting. And as Deuteronomy 3:24 tells us, *"Oh Lord God, You have begun to show Your servant Your greatness and Your mighty hand, for what god is there in heaven or on earth who can do anything like Your works and Your mighty deeds."* Nothing is impossible with you.

Journal Entry March 15, 2021

"May I never boast except in the cross of our Lord Jesus Christ, through which the world has been crucified to me, and I to the world" (Gal. 6:14).

"From now on, let no one cause me trouble, for I bear on my body the marks of Jesus" (Gal. 6:17).

What does it mean to 'bear on my body' the marks of Jesus?

He was flogged for my healing. His back wore the lashes of a thousand sins meant for me, of a million sins meant for all mankind, of that sin nature inherited from Adam. With each stripe that ripped his flesh, He bled for every pain, every sorrow, every disease, and every illness that I have been delivered from. When I feel burdens placed upon my back, Jesus has already carried it. When I feel the sting of others' harshness, Jesus has already bore it. I will remember Christ's suffering for me and know His peace. I praise you Lord for my back and I cast any burden there on you.

Jesus wore a crown of thorns pressed deep into his brow, bleeding eternal-born blood covering my mind and thoughts, delivering me from wrong thinking, debilitating lies and anguishing confusion. He has already transformed my mind from depression, and today He gives me the mind of Christ once more. I praise you Lord for my mind, renewed, restored, and delivered, set free and at peace.

Jesus freely and willingly allowed those He created and loved to pound spikes into his hands and the eternal life-saving blood poured down for me. My hands He created to love, to hold a child, to clasp another's hand, to embrace a friend and bring comfort to a fallen world. I praise You Lord for my hands to be yours in the earth.

In the same way those deadly spikes pierced his feet that, only days earlier, were anointed with rich and fragrant perfume by Mary. And his blood poured down on the mercy seat once and for all, delivering all mankind who are willing to follow him. My feet are His blessing to me and those He leads me to, to share the good news of the gospel message of peace. For blessed are the feet that bring good news. I praise you Lord for my feet; may you take me far and wide and give to me new kingdom territory.

And then a soldier pierced His side and the blood poured down for me. So near His heart, He was wounded by the very ones He created and wept for. When my own heart is wounded, I remember him. No crushing heart wound of mine can compare to all that He bore. He keeps my heart softened and burdened for what grieves His Father's heart and His own. Thank you Lord for my heart, may it beat in time with Your own.

Thank you Lord, so I do bear on my body the marks and scars of Jesus and His suffering. When I remember His death and sacrifice, my vision once more comes into alignment with the Father's will and purpose for my life. That is why He calls us to communion and the remembrance of His suffering, remembrance of his blood.

Focus our vision Lord, focus out activity, and focus our very lives. We are never forsaken because Jesus came for us as Savior and He is coming back again. I decree and declare that I am never alone, and the enemy is not able to lie to me about being isolated or forgotten. Jesus experienced that for me when His Father turned away from all the sin of mankind that He bore on the cross. I break off any feelings of abandonment, betrayal, rejection or desertion in Jesus' Name. I am protected by God's loving hand, and He goes with me wherever I am. Christ came for me. On His cross all the burdens of the world are laid, including mine. He has lifted every one of my burdens in His resurrection.

Romans 8:34 states, *"Who is he that condemns? Christ Jesus, who died – more than that, who was raised to life – is at the right hand of God and is also interceding for us."* Help me to remember Lord that the only scars in heaven are yours!

LESSON 6
Abandoning All- No Mixture

Ezekiel 36:25-30 tells us *"I will sprinkle clean water on you, and you will be clean; I will cleanse you from all your impurities and from all your idols. I will give you a new heart and put a new spirit in you; I will remove from you your heart of stone and give you a heart of flesh. And I will put my Spirit in you and move you to follow my decrees and be careful to keep my laws. Then you will live in the land I gave your ancestors; you will be my people, and I will be your God. I will save you from all your uncleanness. I will call for the grain and make it plentiful and will not bring famine upon you. I will increase the fruit of the trees and the crops of the field, so that you will no longer suffer disgrace among the nations because of famine."*

In November of 1995 newspapers reported the story of lotus seeds found in a dry lake bed in China. They were 1,288 years old! Seven of them were obtained by the University of California at Los Angeles. The seeds were germinated, sprouted, and a plant grew from them. They are thought to be the oldest seeds ever germinated.

If a seed can hold life for 1,288 years, who can doubt the possibility of a bodily resurrection? How pertinent is the illustration the apostle Paul chose of planting, germination, and growth to describe the resurrection of the dead. I Corinthians 15:42 tells us, *"It is the same way for the resurrection of the dead. Our earthly bodies, which die and decay, will be different when they are resurrected, for they will never die."*

I am cleansed and planted by His hand, nurtured by His Spirit, growing by His will, and bearing fruit for His purpose, having an aroma of His love. Let's study this out:

Cleansed by a Holy God

Ezekiel 36:25 tells us *"I will sprinkle clean water on you, and you will be clean; I will cleanse you from all your impurities and from all your idols."*

God's desire for you includes: freedom, cleansing, a new, not remodeled, heart and spirit, His own Spirit within you to enable you to obey Him. His will for each of us is a personal relationship with Him in salvation, a renewed mind through sanctification, and even prosperity in His kingdom as He consecrates us for his service. We are not citizens of this world, our citizenship is in another kingdom that can be accepted only through our hearts. God removes our impurities, our heart of stone, our uncleanness and our disgrace. In all of this God's holy name is glorified because our transformed lives now reflect His glory. Check out the 'Way of the Heart Map' on page 119, and begin to consider where your struggles remain.

During the seventy years of exile, the Hebrew prophet Ezekiel was captive in Babylon. Nebuchadnezzar was king at the time. Ezekiel saw Judah's sin and the punishment caused by forsaking the LORD God. Ezekiel 18:4 states, *"The soul that sins will surely die."* Paul had a similar thought in the NT when he said, *"The wages of sin is death,"* in Romans 6:23. Ezekiel 36:23 states, *"Then the nations will know that I am the LORD, declares the Sovereign LORD, when I am proved holy through you before their eyes."*

- Consider the words "proved holy through you before their eyes". What does this mean?

Read these Scriptures about 'being cleansed by His hand': (Take notes)

    Hebrews 10:27
    Acts 22:16
    I Peter 3:21
    John 3:5
    Galatians 3:27
    Titus 3:5
    I John 1:9
    Psalm 51:10
    I Thessalonians 43:5
    Ephesians 5:26
    Ezekiel 36:25

- How does God cleanse us?

- What should our responses to God be in the cleansing process?

Read these Scriptures about 'being planted by His hand': (Take notes regarding Israel and your own life.)

    2 Samuel 7:10
    Psalm 44:2
    Psalm 80:9
    2 Kings 19:30
    Isaiah 27:6
    Isaiah 37:31
    Psalm 92:12-13
    Jeremiah 1:10
    Hosea 7:12
    Amos 9:15

Choose one of the above Scripture references and research that chapter or section of Scripture. Be prepared to share in your group what you have learned.

Zephaniah 3:17 tells us, *"The LORD your God is with you, he is mighty to save. He will take great delight in you, he will quiet you with his love, he will rejoice over you with singing."*

Daffodils are the first to arrive in spring. They are sunshine yellow, bow their heads, come back each year, have endurance and perseverance, multiply like crazy, are beautiful and bright, they are hardy and are perennials. Why are there not more of them in our gardens? We either never planted them, they have too much shade, or we consider them too much work. We might be too busy. Inside each of us is a garden of our soul. The most vibrant flower we can grow there is our faith. Yet sometimes I have to ask, where is my faith? Have you ever asked that question? We may let unanswered prayers rob us of faith. Or our lack of prioritizing our faith prevent its growth. It may be the darkness of a heart, not yet surrendered, or our will, that hinders the growth of faith in us. Robbed, prevented, hindered; we know the author of those things is Satan! With God's help let us grow our faith today and every day!

Planted by His Hand

Ezekiel 36:26 is a divine revelation of truth of being planted by God's hand, as it states, *"I will give you a new heart and put a new spirit in you; I will remove from you your heart of stone and give you a heart of flesh."*

I want us to look to the second epistle of Peter and see what God's word has to say about our faith and its growth in us toward maturity. Just a brief overview first. The first letter of Peter was to explain the Christian way of living in exile, especially in an oppressive situation. Living in a faith-challenged world, Peter's first letter is filled with words of encouragement and promises of strength and hope and glory. The second letter warned against the many variations on the gospel, and urged believers to cling to the truths they had been taught. His second epistle was a warning against false teachers who infiltrate God's people and lead them astray. While the first letter addresses the external battles we face, the second addresses the internal battles of the mind. Specifically, it speaks of the battle against diverting our attention from the one true God and the gospel. It addresses the truths of the new heart and spirit He gave us. It's a war cry against the lies we believe. We cling to lies instead of allowing God to remove our hearts of stone. The opening verses in second Peter therefore are quite profound in telling us a critical spiritual truth regarding the divine nature that is ours:

> *His divine power has given us **everything we need** for life and godliness through our knowledge of him who called us by his own glory and goodness. Through these he has given us his very great and precious promises, so that through them you may **participate in the divine nature** and escape the corruption in the world caused by evil desires. For this very reason, make every effort to add to your faith goodness; and to goodness, knowledge; and to knowledge, self-control; and to self-control, perseverance; and to perseverance, godliness; and to godliness, brotherly kindness; and to brotherly kindness, love. For if you possess these qualities in increasing measure, they will keep you from being ineffective and unproductive in your knowledge of our Lord Jesus Christ (2 Peter 1:3-8).*

And in I John 5:4 we read, *"For everyone born of God overcomes the world."*

It is God's divine power that gives us everything we need as we participate in his divine nature. Some of us want everything we need for life and godliness, but are not that sure about participating fully in his divine nature. We like our earthly nature more. The basis for Christian growth is found in 2 Peter 1:3, *"His divine power has given us everything we need for life."* We need to understand the Source is always God's Spirit in us. We have obtained this precious faith, this new nature, by God's very DNA. Through the power of this new nature in union with the Holy Spirit, we can live as Jesus: a holy, powerful, and extraordinary life, doing the works He did and bearing great fruit. In Eph. 2:8, we read, *"For by grace are ye saved through faith; and that not of yourselves; it is the gift of God:"* No wonder then that Peter calls it "precious faith".

In I John 3:9 we learn that *"Whosoever is born of God does not commit sin; for his seed remains in him, and he cannot sin, because he is born of God."* This means we cannot continually sin. The word 'seed' is from the Greek word sperma (sperm). God plants the seed of His Word, which is Jesus Christ in your life, should you not then become more like Christ? Our active participation in God's divine nature becomes our spiritual heritage that we are to then walk in. In I Peter 1:23 we learn that Peter referred to this miraculous event when he wrote that you are *"...born not of corruptible seed, but of incorruptible, by the Word of God, which lives and abides forever."*

However, there is a way that we can receive more faith if we desire; we return to the source, God Himself! We can ask and pray for more faith, and we learn in the Word that it comes by hearing the Word of God. What amazing grace we have been afforded. This amazing grace is accessed through faith. Faith is the conduit that transports grace into our lives. If the only faith we have is for being forgiven of our sins, then we live largely fruitless and defeated lives. This is just the first step. The second step is faith for achieving godliness and a pure life. But we must not stop there! For if that is all the further we get in our faith, we might find ourselves held back by obstacles and adversities that prevent us from reaching those in need of the kingdom's power. However, if we have faith to be forgiven, live godly lives, and receive all the spiritual blessings God has provided for us in Christ, then we can accomplish what we have been charged to do: *"Live just as Jesus Christ did"* (I John 2:6), and bring hope and salvation to those in need.

"This is love for God: to obey his commands. And his commands are not burdensome, for everyone born of God overcomes the world. This is the victory that has overcome the world, even our faith. Who is it that overcomes the world? Only he who believes that Jesus is the Son of God" (I John 5:3-5).

So what are the means by which we find this growth operating in our lives? The Word of God in 2 Peter 1: 2-4 teaches…*"through our knowledge of him who called us by his own glory and goodness. Through these he has given us his very great and precious promises, so that through them you may participate in the divine nature."* We grow through the knowledge of God, and of Jesus our Lord. Jesus lived on this earth with a focused mission. He came with a purpose and cause. *"Let us go into the next town that I may preach there also, because for this purpose I have come forth"* (Mark 1:38). *"For this cause I was born, and for this cause I have come into the world, that I should bear witness to the truth"* (John 18:37). Our purpose is the same and that is to bear witness to the truth.

Jesus' most amazing statement before his ascension, *"As the Father has sent Me, I also send you"* (John 20:21) It is a cosmic lie that says we cannot live holy lives. In other words: "As I came for a cause and a purpose- to bear witness of truth, to bear eternal fruit, and to destroy the works of the devil- so I'm sending you." We are commissioned by Jesus Himself to access God's grace to live extraordinary lives and bring forth eternal fruit and destroy the works of the devil. Hebrews 6:11 tells us, *"No one can please God without faith"*. Another translations says it is impossible to please God without faith- IMPOSSIBLE! Faith seems downright critical, don't you think?

No faith equals no grace and no ability to please God. The apostles struggled with this as well and Jesus was always saying, *"Ye of little faith."*(Matt. 8:26). Finally the apostles cried out *"The apostles said to the Lord, "Increase our faith!"* (Luke 17:5). Finally the apostles were aware of its importance and Jesus responded- *"If you have faith as a mustard seed, you can say to this mulberry tree, be pulled up by the roots and be planted in the sea"* (Luke 17:6). Faith originates from what seems insignificant. The extraordinary starts out with His Word, which is the seed.

Our Father Gardener plants a seed of his word and truth in our lives. That seed, the word of God, has everything it needs to grow into the parent plant as it is planted in good soil, watered and given light. The key is getting his Word into our inner being. *"For with the heart one believes"* (Rom. 10:10). Our heart is the seat of our belief, so this is where the seed must be planted. Jesus discussed this pivotal truth in the story of the sower and it is such a critical story Jesus said, *"If you don't understand this story, you won't understand any others"* (Mark 4:13).

Jesus tells us in Luke 8:11 *"If you have faith as a mustard seed."* He's referring to the Word of God the Holy Spirit speaks to our hearts from Scripture or other sources that line up with Scripture. A seed contains everything needed to fulfill its destiny; all that is needed is the soil of our heart. That is why it is important to have a tender heart not a hard heart. The heart condition of believers limits God's kingdom work on this earth if the Word of God is not permitted to grow and produce fruit in our lives.

Jesus had no lack of faith. *"Behold, I have come- in the volume of the book it is written of me – to do your will, O God"* (Heb. 10:7). Just as Jesus had books written about His destiny in heaven, so do each of us. Jesus fulfilled God's desires perfectly, but when He returned to the Father, He left the task of completing the work with us. We are the ecclesia, the Church remnant. Now the will of God, bearing witness of the truth and destroying the works of the devil, can be accomplished. It is not just through one man, Jesus Christ, but through His entire body, the multitude of believers. The only condition is that we must cooperate; it begins in our hearts.

In Luke 8:12 the seeds land on the path, the devil takes it away. Satan does not want his work destroyed so he tempts us to use human reasoning or stand on the erroneous beliefs we tend to cling to. Satan is subtle and crafty and his goal is to make God's Word appear abnormal, and the world's wisdom normal. Good is considered evil and evil is considered good in the world systems; we see it every day!

In Luke 8:13 the seed falls on rocky ground. People gladly hear the message and accept it but they have no roots in prayer, Bible reading or fellowship and when life gets hard they give up. It is an important and key thought we must consider; to have no roots. Seeds are a miracle of life so it is an important analogy the Lord has given us. When roots go deep they can actually erode and break apart rock. The Word does the same things in the hardness of a heart. Everyone experiences a critical belief period where they are tempted to believe in an adversity more than in God's Word. That is why we are told to rejoice in tribulation. Rejoicing keeps us close to the heart of God, and keeps us from opening the door to bitterness, fear, or disillusionment with God and others. We find revelation of Jesus in the Word. Everything a Christian needs to grow and develop into what God wants them to be is found there. Jesus had all He needed to fulfill the Father's will, and so do you and I.

Nurtured by His Spirit

Ezekiel 36:27 states, *"And I will put my Spirit in you and move you to follow my decrees and be careful to keep my laws."*

We have probably all heard of the place called Death Valley. Normally it is barren and forbidding, but every once and a while it explodes with color. Millions of wildflowers emerge from the ground and make the desert floor as beautiful as a painting. Where did the flowers come from? They were actually there all the time. They were in the ground in seed form, waiting to be nurtured and released. When the seeds receive the right amount of sun and rain, they explode with life. Out of our desert experiences, with God's help, come life and great beauty. This is beautifully expressed in Isaiah 61:11 where it says, *"For as the soil makes the sprout come up and a garden causes seeds to grow, so the Sovereign LORD will make righteousness and praise spring up before all nations."* God is the one who plants Holy Spirit in us. Holy Spirit then directs us to follow his ways.

In the world there is corruption, death, decay, and waste, and this results from "lust" which the desires and appetites of our old nature crave. God uses words to paint pictures of what He desires on the screen of our imagination. Since the enemy also wants to contend for the screen of our hearts and minds, it's the spiritual war zone of our lives. What we allow to fill that screen is what will come forth from our lives. The words we hear and heed on a daily basis will paint pictures on our heart's and mind's screen. That's why Jesus said, *"Consider carefully what you hear,"* he continued. *"With the measure you use, it will be measured to you—and even more"* (Mark 4:24). We must actively participate with the Spirit God places in us, to move and follow His decrees and keep His laws. What are you listening to? Satan's list of visuals includes failure, defeat, poverty, sickness, hopelessness, inability and so on. The list is endless. Worry and fear are the biggest! God does the opposite. His words are always of hope, restoration, redemption, life, joy, peace, ability, health, wholeness, and confidence in Him. His Spirit guides us in this.

Abraham and Sarah were promised a child whose descendants would outnumber the stars in the sky and the sand on the seashore. Romans 4:18 tells us of Abraham – *"Who against hope believed in hope, that he might become the father of many nations, according to that which was spoken, so shall thy seed be."* The first hope is natural hope, the other is God's kind of hope, which is the second one Paul mentions. The word hope in the Bible is defined as "a confident expectation", not the "maybe so" definition most of us use for hope. *"Now faith is the substance of things hoped for"* (Hebrews 11:1). Hope is the picture painted by God's word on the screen and garden of our minds and hearts, and faith gives substance to it and brings it to reality. Many struggle with faith because they lack hope. Hope is a blueprint for the building materials of faith. We need to fight with all our heart, mind and soul against this "corruption" with all God's "exceeding great and precious promises". As we come to know and desire God's Word and his many promises, the journey of faith towards holiness has a cleansing effect. We begin to grow and develop as Christians when we apply the principles of God's Word in our lives. We then escape the corruption around us, as we take an active role in pushing back the gates of hell. God has a new heart and new spirit for us that only He can give, but we must receive it and walk in it.

Growing by His Will -A New Heart and Spirit

Ezekiel 36:28-29 tells us *"Then you will live in the land I gave your ancestors; you will be my people, and I will be your God. I will save you from all your uncleanness, I will call for the grain and make it plentiful and will not bring famine upon you."*

> *For this very reason, make every effort to add to your faith goodness; and to goodness, knowledge; and to knowledge, self-control; and to self-control, perseverance; and to perseverance, godliness; and to godliness, brotherly kindness; and to brotherly kindness, love. For if you possess these qualities in increasing measure, they will keep you from being ineffective and unproductive in your knowledge of our Lord Jesus Christ. (2 Peter 1:5-8)*

The nature of Christian growth is practically detailed in 2 Peter 1:5-8. To live in the land God is giving us in His Kingdom we must have this Scripture truly formed in us, truly built up in us, truly transforming us. This will allow us to live in the land of God's kingdom. When it says "...giving all diligence, add to your faith ..." this does not mean that we can add to it by our own strength or ability, but only through the grace of God. It is also not a suggestion. 'Making every effort' is not an apathetic or complacent stance, but rather one of sincere and dedicated action and diligence. Since our faith is the foundation upon which we are to build, if it is improperly laid, then what we try to build on top of it will not stand. *"By the grace God has given me, I laid a foundation as a wise builder, and someone else is building on it. But each one should build with care. For no one can lay any foundation other than the one already laid, which is Jesus Christ"* (1 Cor. 3:10-11).

So as we build our faith, there are seven floors or stories if you will. The first, we are to add to our faith virtue; this is moral excellence and uprightness. We are called to walk upright before God and by applying the Word to our lives we can be virtuous. The second story is to virtue add knowledge. Ignorance never reflects spiritual growth. 1 Peter 2:2, *"As newborn babes, desire the sincere milk of the Word, that ye may grow thereby"*. And in 2 Peter 3:18 we are commanded to *grow in grace and in knowledge of our Lord*. The third story of our spiritual faith is to add to knowledge temperance, or self-control to every aspect of our lives. This includes our speech, our habits, our conduct, and even our very thinking. The fourth story is to add to temperance patience, which is endurance under trials. This is a steadfastness that endures even in the midst of great trials, suffering and temptation. On the fifth floor of our faith building we are to add to patience godliness, which is fearing God and doing what pleases Him. Our attitudes and thoughts ever turned toward Him. Sixth, to godliness brotherly kindness, for non-believers will know us by our love one toward another. It literally means to show kindness to all those in Christ. And seventh, to brotherly kindness charity, a deep love for all those God created with his love divinely infused in us. To see others as God sees them. So if this is the nature of Christian growth, how are we doing? Does our life reflect these characteristics? Let no doubt be found in us as to who we belong to and the God we serve. The will of God nurtures us and longs to bless us with the good things in life.

Bearing Fruit for His Purpose

Ezekiel 36:30 reads, *"I will increase the fruit of the trees and the crops of the field, so that you will no longer suffer disgrace among the nations because of famine."*

"For if you possess these qualities in increasing measure, they will keep you from being ineffective and unproductive in your knowledge of our Lord Jesus Christ" (2 Peter 1:8).

Possessing the qualities we studied above will bring fruitfulness and Jesus has made that very clear that He desires that we bear much fruit. So what fruit am I producing? Not sure about you, but when I read Proverbs 31:25-31, I'm challenged to do better:

> *"She is clothed with strength and dignity; she can laugh at the days to come. She speaks with wisdom, and faithful instruction is on her tongue. She watches over the affairs of her household and does not eat the bread of idleness. Her children arise and call her blessed; her husband also, and he praises her: "Many women do noble things, but you surpass them all." Charm is deceptive, and beauty is fleeting; but a woman who fears the LORD is to be praised. Honor her for all that her hands have done, and let her works bring her praise at the city gate."*

I am not complete in this description, but I will fear the Lord until Holy Spirit in me perfects all that is possible. I am encouraged that nothing is impossible for my God, and He completes the good work started in us.

Proverbs 11:30 tells us, *"The fruit of the righteous is a tree of life, and he who wins souls is wise."*

First of all, God empowers us for the work He calls us to. If someone would have told me that I would minister to women in prison 20 years ago as an elementary school teacher, I would not have believed them. God had plans I knew not of. Secondly, God gives us assurance. So many people ask me how they can know for sure that they are in God's will. Here is one way, determine to live a godly life and watch what happens. Jesus is the Vine, and we are both the branches and its fruit. If the fruit of our lives falls to the ground, then new seeds are planted. When we stay connected to Christ, His life giving flow saturates our life. We become ripe fruit in the Kingdom, and then die to self for the seed within to be planted anew in another's life. We give of ourselves to others as we die to self, but God produces fruit in another's life because of our obedience to him. Most Christians who have trouble with assurance, either for salvation or God's will, need to spend more time in the Word of God, and then start living their lives in accordance with His Book! He guides us one day at a time, gives manna one day at a time, and equips for service one day at a time. He enables us, as we step out in obedience, one day at a time. Then Jesus gives us a front row stance to witness signs, wonders and miracles because that is what the kingdom life is like.

Having an Aroma of His Love

Nature wonderfully testifies that adverse conditions are often valuable in the development of some types of trees and plants. While fire is one of the forest's great enemies, it actually helps certain kinds of seeds to grow. The cones of some pines do not open until they are touched by the flames. Likewise, the Christian's faith and character are often strengthened by life's trials.

God's desire for you includes: freedom, cleansing, a new–not remodeled heart and spirit, His own Spirit within you to enable you to obey Him, a personal relationship with Him, a renewed mind, and even prosperity in God's kingdom. You are planted by God's own hand

and the seed of His Word is planted in your heart. You are nurtured by Holy Spirit as you allow the screen of your mind and heart to receive the Word of God on a daily basis, changing your very nature. You are empowered by Holy Spirit to live an extraordinary life producing fruit for His kingdom, and having an aroma of His love. We are not citizens of this world, our citizenship is in another kingdom that can be accepted only through our hearts. God removes our impurities, our heart of stone, our uncleanness and our disgrace. In all of this, God's holy name is glorified because our transformed lives now reflect His glory.

God can be your ABBA Father if this is the first time his Word has been planted in your heart. He is only a prayer away. Today ask Jesus Christ to come into your life. Receive Him as your Lord and Savior, and let God become your heavenly ABBA Father, so you may know the fullness of is love and begin your journey of faith. Perhaps you are struggling with godliness and holiness, His Spirit is available for you today to give you greater faith, and help you become victorious in those areas of your life that you need to surrender. Access His abundant grace. Just ask him, He hears your heart. And those of you who are wanting to move from a place of ordinary to a place of extraordinary living for Christ, die to self and step out in obedience receiving all the Lord has for you today. Just as Peter stepped out of the boat, sometimes we need to step out of our comfort zones, and practice that heavenly walk, keeping our eyes focused on Christ. Jesus will build our faith as we ask Him to. His divine power has given us everything we need for life and godliness through our knowledge of Him who called us by His own glory and goodness.

Zephaniah 3:17 says *"The LORD your God is with you, he is mighty to save. He will take great delight in you, he will quiet you with his love, he will rejoice over you with singing."*

Are you a Christian? Do you have the assurance of your salvation?

Are you a growing Christian? If not, what will you do about it?

How much time and attention will you give to the nurturing of your faith by abiding in the Word of God?

Are you bearing fruit?

How much time will you give to prayer and asking for more faith and more of the Holy Spirit in you?

If there is a need in your life today, surrender all to the One who surrendered all for you.

Our courage for the journey so often fails because we have lost our hope of heaven, the consummation of our true love story. The higher story will be fulfilled, remember this is not all there is. Once the enemy of our souls is defeated once and for all, and Jesus judges the nations, God will establish His everlasting kingdom and rule for all eternity. Jerusalem will be the golden holy city, and the enemies will never again pass through her gates. The thorns and briars of the enemy's lies will no longer have a foothold in our lives. They need not have one now either. Are you encouraged today? We have so much to anticipate! The God of the universe will reign supreme. All sorrow and suffering will end. And peace and blessing will be our inheritance and we will walk beside majestic rivers of His love. He sings over us with His love. When the trumpet sounds may we be ready!

Spend some time with the Lord meditating on which areas of your life still need to be surrendered. Remember, this cannot be a once and done activity, we must surrender daily to the will and purposes of God. Use the 'Way of the Heart' map on the next page to help you.

THE WAY OF THE HEART

Galatians 6:8 – "For he who sows to his own flesh will from the
flesh reap decay and ruin and destruction...

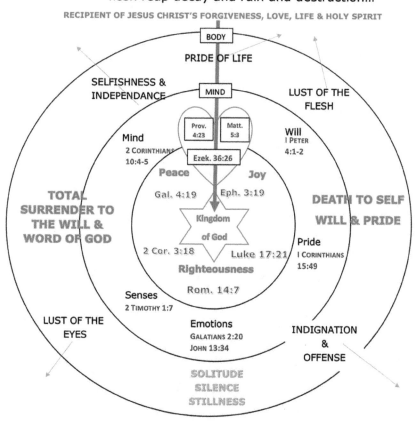

...but he who sows to the Spirit will from the Spirit reap eternal life."

#6. Another obstacles that keeps us from enjoying a right relationship with the Father as His son or daughter is thinking we have abandoned all but really have not.

Our courage for this journey called life so often fails because we have lost our hope of heaven, the ultimate consummation of our love story as the bride of Christ. The higher story will be fulfilled, this is not all there is! But our surrendered heart to Jesus means everything. We have to be all in. There is no room for compromise, no room for apathy, no room for mixture with the world, and no room for continual conscious sin in our lives. Once the enemy of our souls is defeated once and for all and Jesus judges the nations, He will establish His everlasting kingdom and rule for all eternity. Jesus called us 'living stones' so as we build our faith, make every effort to "*add to your faith goodness; and to goodness, knowledge; and to knowledge, self-control; and to self-control, perseverance; and to perseverance, godliness; and to godliness, brotherly kindness; and to brotherly kindness, love*" (2 Peter 1:5-7). Jerusalem will be the golden holy city and the enemies will never again pass through her gates. The thorns and briars of the enemy's lies will no longer have a foothold in our lives. They need not have a position now either. Surrender all to the One who surrendered all for you. Sacrifice all to the One who sacrificed all for you. Die to self and live to eternal life. But for the joy set before Him, Jesus endured the cross. What must you endure today? Your choices determine your destiny and your eternity. I pray you are encouraged today. We have so much to anticipate! The God of the universe will reign supreme. All sorrow and suffering will end. And peace and blessing will be our inheritance and we will walk beside majestic rivers of His love. He sings over us with His love.

Prayer to **Adonai, Master over All**

You are **Adonai, Master over All**, the One who wears the Victor's Crown and I pledge my undying devotion to You. You have called me out of any mixture with this world. You call me anew and afresh to come and receive a new sword from You. You have more for me and so I come; to be restored, equipped anew, to go out yet again and face the giants. This time though, I go out in greater power, in greater anointing and in greater strength than ever before for You, Immanuel, are ever with me. Forgive me Lord for all the times I have not surrendered all. Strengthen me to be diligent in possessing the characteristics of Your nature in greater measure. The sword of Your Word is mighty to the tearing down of strongholds in my life, but if I am not reading and meditating on it, the enemy comes to steal, kill and destroy. He has already taken so much from me. Rise up in me Holy Spirit to go into the enemy's camp and take back what he has stolen from me. I declare and decree I will hold the territory the Lord has given me. I declare and decree that I will take new territory in His Name. I declare and decree that faith, goodness, knowledge, self-control, perseverance, godliness, brotherly kindness, and love will grow in me in greater measure. Be my Master over all: over all sickness, doubt, fear, relationships, worry, and all the attacks of the enemy. Let there be no mixture in me with this world and its lies. You have so much more for me and so I come; to be restored, equipped anew, to go out yet again and face the giants. This time though, I go out in greater power, in greater anointing and in greater strength than ever before for You Adonai are ever with me.

BROKEN FOR HIS GLORY

Chapter VII

*When I have come completely to the end of myself and the crushing weight of brokenness, You, **Jehovah Uzzi are My Strength** equipping me in your almighty power.*

The LORD (Jehovah) is my strength (Uzzi) and my shield. My heart trusts in Him, and I am helped. Therefore my heart exults, and with my song I shall thank Him (Ps. 28:7).

The Lord is close to the brokenhearted and saves those who are crushed in spirit (Ps. 34:18).

For I know the plans I have for you," declares the Lord, "plans to prosper you and not to harm you, plans to give you hope and a future (Jer. 29:11).

Broken Before a Holy God

Aglatha, AJ (not her real name) to her friends, referred to herself as the Black Queen. She knew her royal identity in Christ. She called Jesus her boyfriend. She knew she was part of the bride of Christ. She called me her friend, and the Holy Spirit united us in learning and service past all racial and socio-economic differences. AJ was a Jesus transformed and delivered addict from the streets, and when she met Christ, she was one of my best friends. She was broken for God's glory! I only wrote a poem for one other person and that was my Dad. The following is her eulogy and the poem attributed to her. I share it both as a tribute to her and as an example of how God can change one life that has been broken before Him. Your brokenness has purpose and can be transformed by our living Christ.

I met AJ in 2006 at a spiritual retreat in Valley Forge. When I first met her I remember thinking 'What a character!' She was bold, brassy and crass at times. She spoke truth with a street sense I found quite honest and refreshing. She said it like it was and centered in on the heart of every issue; sometimes embarrassingly so. Many did not understand her spiritual metaphors, but I found them fascinating and profound. Over the past several years she participated in one of my home groups and served alongside our team in the prison ministry. Her love for Jesus radiated from her countenance with the fragrance of Christ, and she was quite an influence wherever she went. The fragrance of Christ poured forth from her speech moment by moment. She praised God with a life of worship in all the years I knew her. The kingdom of heaven can only be preached by those who have learned to prize the authority of that kingdom and humble themselves before the One who saved them. AJ did exactly that. When she spoke to the ladies at the prison both in services and during one-on-one's, the Holy Spirit's power was evident in and through her as women gave their hearts to Christ. Many were delivered from many of the same struggles God had delivered her from. Spiritual chains were broken when AJ was around because she carried the glory and power of our living God. When I shared one Monday at Bible study with the women at the prison of AJ's influence, and that she had passed on to glory, many of the women knew her and wept. A young woman came up to me afterwards and in tears thanked me for sharing because she said AJ led her to Christ. The chaplain later told me that this was the last young woman AJ spoke to at the prison. Wave after wave as ripples in a pond the Word of God will never return void nor will the influence of Christ in one life. AJ lived such a life of influence for Christ. The effects of the Word that AJ sowed into many lives will never be realized this side of heaven, but one day we will share in that glorious tale. The prison team had lost a warrior princess and there will never be another 'Black Queen' (her own title of herself) in our lives quite like her, I am honored to have called her 'Friend'!

<u>Example of Devotion</u>
Her boyfriend was her Jesus
Speaking to her day and night
Her countenance was His Grace
Wrapping her in light

She wore royal robes of righteousness
Given her by the King
Warrior Princess- knowing her call
She wore His signet ring

AJ drank deeply; these living waters
Doing battle in the secret place
Communed behind spiritual veil
She finished well; this life, this race

In the Spirit's realm of love and truth
Her metaphors gave life and breadth
She's dancing streets of glory now

Celebrating eternal life, not death

She loved the broken and the lost
And never tired till the very end
Uniquely fashioned, touching hearts
I'm honored to have called her friend.

Would that a tribute be said of us all. Some of us are broken early in life, others later. But will we hear our Master's voice in the midst of our heartaches? He's fashioning us for His glory. *"Therefore I tell you, her sins, which are many, are forgiven, for she loved much. But to whom little is forgiven, the same loves little"* (Luke 7:47).

Some believers, when they are in a comfortable and sheltered atmosphere of earthly warmth, pleasure, and luxury, they begin to lose their spiritual vitality, if they ever had it. On the other hand, if they are faced with the icy winds of life and chilling temptations, they soon seek God; reviving and renewing their strength and making firm their commitment to Him.

So I praise God for the fiery trials of this world, as they continue to purge me of all earthly affections. God breaks my heart for what breaks His. Sometimes our own children can become idols in our lives. We set them up to fulfill needs in our own hearts that they were never meant to carry. Sometimes we love them too much. Sometimes we expect them to follow a course of our own choosing based on what we know to be true in the Word and in our own experience. And when those things do not happen, our world shifts off its axis.

One of my greatest heartaches came in the midst of an ordinary day at a family dinner with my husband, son, and daughter. The children were transitioning from college and travel to living at home for a few months before going out once more into the world of jobs and responsibilities. All time and seasons stopped as if a Mack truck had entered the room and shifted the heavenlies above our heads, as our world suddenly tilted off its axis. Our children were choosing paths that we had not prayed or dreamed for them. Some of the news that day was against our biblical world view that we had tried to instill in their spirits. My shock and surprise were so great that neither tears nor anger overtook me, just dumb silence and a retreat into new levels of questioning God. The brokenness I was experiencing was reminiscent of past hurts, rejections and loss. Knowing God would sustain us, we chose to continue to love even in our own imperfections and misunderstandings.

Ten years passed of strained visits, very limited conversations, and brief interactions where few true conversations occurred. My husband and I continued to pray and wait on God. God gave my husband and me divine peace. Our beautiful, loving and intelligent precious children had chosen the world's views over God's and ours in what we had tried to teach them. But God continues to give us peace through it all and our love for them is quite sincere. He let us see His heart for the masses; the children He loves and lost to their own choices. It gave us greater passion for the lost. We stand in faith and continue to believe God will transform thinking and soften hearts in all our lives. In the meantime we will serve God and be faithful to what we know to be true. Our lives were forever changed, but we are believing for eternal changes in all of our hearts as we move forward.

I am sure many of my readers know the shocks of life, whether in the death of a loved one, a betrayal of a close friend, a divorce, loss of a job, the rejection of a loved one, the loss of identity of one we love, or any number of sorrows. I have found that the waves of God's grace and poetry within can carry us through. If God brings me to it, God will always bring me through it.

So in all this my faith was actually strengthened, and my husband and I grew closer spiritually. My husband and I were both called out of the churches we had been attending, and began worshiping together at a new church. My God will work all things together for our good and His glory! I believe that with all my heart.

We laid our Isaac down into the arms of our heavenly Father, our sweet Abba. You need to put Isaac on the altar like Abraham; whomever or whatever that may be. God must be your only strength, your only boast, your only solace. Pride in our children can sometimes be a stumbling block that is actually idolatry. We laid all that down. Identify your own Isaac- identity? Security? Gifts? Dreams? People? Children? God must be first!

> *Then God said, "Take your son, your only son, whom you love—Isaac—and go to the region of Moriah. Sacrifice him there as a burnt offering on a mountain I will show you"* (Gen. 22:2).

> *When they reached the place God had told him about, Abraham built an altar there and arranged the wood on it. He bound his son Isaac and laid him on the altar, on top of the wood* (Gen. 22:9).

Brokenness is part of this fallen world and I am sure everyone reading this has examples in their own life. David cried out in Psalm 31:12, *"I am forgotten as a dead man out of mind:*
I am like a broken vessel," but then proclaimed in Psalm 147:3 *"He heals the broken hearted and binds up their wounds."* We do not want the reality of the one without the reality of the other. Healing comes with renewed reality; focusing our consciousness on kingdom issues and promises above the lies and issues of the natural realm. I have seen that the more I live within the definition of myself that I have learned from God, the more I am able to resist definitions and labels imposed on me by others. The truer self is like a shield from heaven to fend off attacks of negativity, lies, and the opinions of others. Attacks of the enemy from both within and without.

Renewed reality takes shape even as we understand that we are Christ's beloved. We learn to leave our failures and own screw-ups at the foot of the cross and take up the clarion call of Isaiah 61:1. *"The Spirit of the Sovereign Lord is on me, because the Lord has anointed me to preach good news to the poor. He has sent me to bind up the broken-hearted, to proclaim freedom for the captives and release from darkness for the prisoner".*

You might be thinking, wait a minute, is not that Scripture talking about Jesus? Yes it is, but it is also talking about you. We have been called to look into the mirror of God's word, and identify and know our identity in Christ: to be formed in Him, to take on His image. That is what true believing is; taking God at his Word and appropriating every promise to our own lives.

To do this we must gaze into the mirror that is Christ. Peter, James, and John were shown the truth of who Jesus was all along on the Mount of Transfiguration. It changed them! I am convinced that gazing into the mirror of God's word, Jesus Himself, will change us too. Only Jesus can show us who we are, so let us gaze at Him.

1 Corinthians 13:12 says, *"For now we see only a reflection as in a mirror; then we shall see face to face. Now I know in part, then I shall know fully even as I am fully known."* Doesn't this make you wonder if you have seen the part we are meant to see? How can we see if we do not look, taste and see that He is good?

We must be open to the Holy Spirit's instruction, *"… for the Holy Spirit will teach you at that time what needs to be said"* (Luke 12:12). God keeps us to be holy. Jesus is the only one who can truly see us clearly and speak truth to us in love. He sees with complete clarity and perfect charity, committed to our transformation into His faithful, untarnished image. It is a process of a lifetime spent seeking His face, receiving His promises, declaring His truth, walking in obedience and receiving His discipline.

> *The sacrifices of God are a broken spirit: a broken and a contrite heart, O God, thou wilt not despise* (Psalms 51:17).

> *Some of you were once like that. But you were cleansed; you were made holy; You were made right with God by*

calling on the name of the Lord Jesus Christ and by the Spirit of our God (I Corinthians 6:11).

LESSON 7

Broken Before a Holy God

Read Matthew 4:1-7

When Jesus was tempted in the desert, He would not assume an identity that was not true. We get the impression there was a cosmic struggle over Jesus' true identity. Have you assumed an identity that is not true; not the one written in the book of heaven about your eternal destiny? Just as if we were on a potter's wheel, we find ourselves 'turned over' again and again until Christ is formed in us; until all parts of ourselves are healed and restored by God. This turning over and over reminds me of a ballerina when she is spinning. She returns to a focal point on each turn so she will not get dizzy. Getting our focal point on Christ is crucial to not spinning out of control in our spiritual lives. Once we stop looking inward at ourselves and begin instead to look outward to Christ and others, then Jesus can help us look at ourselves in the true mirror of His love. It is then we will see a new creation. Our focus will be the image of Christ- familiar, beloved, astonishing, and we will continue to die to self. Our joy will be full!

Read Isaiah 6. When we gaze into the face of God and His Word, it exposes us, it exposes our culture, and it turns us into a world changer.

- Isaiah 6:1 describes what Isaiah saw. Can you recall or describe a time when you truly felt that you 'saw' God in your spirit man?

- What was Isaiah's response in encountering God in this way? (Isaiah 6:5-8)

- In Isaiah 6:9 what message was he to take to the people?

- What is 'the seed' referring to in Isaiah 6:13?

- How can you be a world changer in these times?

As we encounter a Holy God we will end false allegiances because we become what we behold. Beholding Him burns us holy. Has the enemy of your soul been ruling your life, and it has only brought you sorrow, lies, and deception? Perhaps you have been 'beholding' too much of this world's lies, culture, media, deception and lusts.

The Psalmist invites us in Psalm 34:8 *"To taste and see that the Lord is good."* And 1 John 3:2 says, *"We will see Him as He is."* We are cautioned in Proverbs 25; 28 *"He that hath no rule over his own spirit is like a city that is broken down, and without walls."*

- What responsibility do each of us have in 'ruling over our spirit'?

- How do we do this?

- What does 'beholding' God mean to you?

- What are some things you are 'beholding' that need to be eliminated from your life?

Nothing else really matters but Jesus. Have you come to that realization yet? Read these two verses and write what the Lord speaks to your heart below. Sometimes the things that we find so difficult in life that seem to shatter us, are only allowed by a Holy God to get our attention. The result brings us to our knees in repentance so Jesus can be glorified through our lives.

> *Teacher, which is the great commandment in the* Law?" *And he said to him, "You shall love* the Lord your God with all your heart and with all your soul and with all your mind. This is the great and first commandment. And a second is like it: You shall *love your neighbor as yourself* (Matthew 22:37-39).

> *Therefore, this is what the Sovereign Lord says: Look! I am placing a foundation stone in Jerusalem, a firm and tested stone. It is a precious cornerstone that is safe to build on. Whoever believes need never be shaken* (Isaiah 28:16).

Your thoughts:

Noticing His Presence all around is a learned skill. To gaze at Jesus is to penetrate with the heart what is ordinarily missed by the eye. It is to see in the unseen what is felt in the spirit. It is to awaken our mind and intellect to being conformed to the mind of Christ by the Word of God. We can gaze upon the Lord in our remorsefulness, act with a confession, and then bow in receiving forgiveness. We can gaze upon the Lord in confusion, act with trust, and hold fast to His promises. We can gaze upon the Lord overcome with emotion, act with praise and worship, and fall before Him in awe. We can gaze upon the Lord in our brokenness, ask for more faith, and watch and see what the Lord will do as He holds us close. Our problem many times is we are relying on learned skills and patterns of this world, keeping our focus on what is seen. We experience remorsefulness, confusion, emotion and broken-ness and forget to take them to the throne of grace. We want to handle it all ourselves and all it causes is pain and regret. Let's take serious what Jesus knew so well:

> *My Father is always at his work to this very day, and I, too, am working. I tell you the truth, the Son can do nothing by himself; he can do only what he sees his Father doing, because whatever the Father does the Son also does. For the Father loves the Son and shows him all he does. Yes, to your amazement he will show him even greater things than these (John 5:17, 19-20).*

We are equipped for the battle as God delivers us from wrong thinking, lifts us out of self-centeredness, and gracefully by His Spirit helps keep our gaze on Him.

> *Put on all of God's armor so that you will be able to stand firm against all strategies of the devil. For we are not fighting against flesh and blood enemies, but against evil rulers and authorities of the unseen world, against mighty*

powers in this dark world and against evil spirits in the heavenly places. Therefore, put on every piece of God's armor so you will be able to resist the enemy in the time of evil. Then after the battle you will still be standing firm. Stand your ground, putting on the belt of truth and the body armor of God's righteousness. For shoes, put on the peace that comes from the Good News so that you will be fully prepared. In addition to all of these hold up the shield of faith to stop the fiery arrows of the devil. Put on salvation as your helmet, and take the sword of the Spirit, which is the word of God (Ephesians 6:10-17).

* What aspects of brokenness, trust, restoration and gazing into the face of Christ do you find yourself in during this current season?

* How can God use you in this period of life?

I hope you realize that God sanctifies our sorrows not only for our restoration but for His own glory and the restoration of others.

Meditatively read these Scriptures:

And the vessel that he made of clay was marred in the hand of the potter: so he made it again another vessel, as seemed good to the potter to make it (Jeremiah 18:4).

From the beginning God chose you to be saved through the sanctifying work of the Spirit and through belief in the truth (2 Thessalonians 2:1).

And when he had given thanks, he broke it, and said, Take, eat: this is my body, which is broken for you, this do in remembrance of me (1 Corinthians 11:24).

Our Lord was broken, but through his brokenness, the greatest blessing of them all, salvation, was made available for all mankind. Our trials were meant to fashion us into a vessel God can use to bring Him glory and draw others to Himself. Being broken before a holy God is better than being broken without His presence in your life. From 2020-2022 there were more teenagers admitted for suicidal thoughts to our hospitals than at any other time. Our world is broken and the disciples of Christ have a mission to reach a lost world with the good news of the gospel. Our hope is in Christ, not this world or its systems. Halleluiah Lord!!!

Charles Spurgeon, the noted nineteenth-century preacher, once asked, *"Is it not a curious thing that, whenever God means to make a man great, he always breaks him in pieces first?"*[12]

As I began this book for the Lord, I was not sure of its eventual scope. I do know that the Lord has called me to write it, so I began in obedience with words of faith. Just as David cried out in Psalm 31:12 where he said, *"I am forgotten as a dead man out of mind, I have become as broken pottery."* So too I have been in that place, more than once, where that was the cry of my heart. And just as he proclaimed healing in Psalm 147:3 *"He heals the broken hearted and binds up their wounds"*, so too He has done for me multiple times. I am sure many of us can relate because brokenness is one way for the Lord God to get our attention. Should you still be in a place of brokenness, and have not realized the peace of healing in your inner being, please consider that God is more than able to see you through. This reading may be for you in your journey of faith.

Have you ever wondered why? I am sure you have, just as the millions who have come before you have, and the millions who will come after you. It is a two-year olds' favorite word! The God of the universe has planted inside each of us a wonder and questioning heart as to why we are here, who we are to be, and how we are to spend our days on this earth. His plan is to have relationship with us, so the void in the center of our soul could find its satisfaction. The void and emptiness of spirit was placed there by our Creator to only be filled by His Spirit. Is it no wonder that it cannot be filled until it is filled with God Himself, not partially but fully and completely?

Oswald Chambers was right when he said, *"If we are ever going to be made into wine, we will have to be crushed—you cannot drink grapes. Grapes become wine only when they have been squeezed."*[13]

"The sacrifices of God are a broken spirit: a broken and a contrite heart, O God, thou wilt not despise" (Psalms 51:17).

> *For this is what the high and lofty one says— he who lives forever, whose name is holy: "I live in a high and holy place, but also with him who is contrite and lowly in spirit, to revive the spirit of the lowly and to revive the heart of the contrite* (Isaiah 57:15).

1. If we need to **put Isaac on the altar** like Abraham, then who or what is our Isaac? (Read Gen. 22:2-9)

2. If we need to **throw down our staff** like Moses, then what is in your hand? (Read Exodus 7:8-19)

3. If we need to **burn our plowing equipment** like Elisha, then what do you need to burn? (Read 1 Kings 19:19-21)

4. If we need to **climb a cliff** like Jonathon, then what cliff do you need to climb? (Read 1 Samuel 14:1-14)

5. If we need to **get out of the boat** to walk on water like Peter, then what step of obedience or trust do you need to make? (Read Matthew 14)

#7. Another obstacle that keeps us from enjoying a right relationship with the Father as His son or daughter are the crushing weights of brokenness.

So now that we know we are not alone in our brokenness, perhaps we can get some divine perspective on not allowing it to keep us from a right relationship with God and others. Once we realize that Christ has been broken for us, and that God does not despise our own brokenness, we can gaze into the mirror of His love. Within God's Word we will find both restoration and relief. Sometimes we remain in our broken state, and sometimes it actually gets worse. Perhaps it is because we do the same things over and over again. It may be time for you to do something different. To yield a different result perhaps daily Bible reading, praise, and prayer will kick start you out of your cycle of defeat. Find an accountability partner or mentor, and attend a Bible teaching fellowship or Bible study. If those are already a part of your habit, praise God! If you find you are doing those things and still feel overpowered by broken relationships, finances, or circumstances perhaps a Christian counselor might be in order. Possibly, we are holding on too tightly to something or someone that God is asking us to let go of and let Him deal with it or them. We cannot change others; that is God's job. We can only change ourselves. Finding our victory in Christ alone takes some effort on our part to weed through the entanglements the enemy of our soul tries to bind us with. Christ has set us free, but the bird cage door can be open and we are still sitting inside the cage of the enemy's lies. Explore some answers by gazing into Jesus' face, because once we stop looking 'to' ourselves, then Jesus can help us to look 'at' ourselves in the true mirror of His image.

PRAYER TO JEHOVAH UZZI, MY STRENGTH

My Jehovah Uzzi, You truly are my strength whenever I come to the end of myself. I found it is not just once that You have done this, but You bring me to the end of myself often to keep me humble. You long for me to know my brokenness, and help me walk in Holy Spirit fully in the life You called me to. You alone are able to shine your magnificent light in me as I yield my brokenness and weakness. It is from those shattered fragments that my life is rebuilt into a vessel of grace. Thank you for loving me so much Lord and equipping me with Holy Spirit's almighty power and strength. Help me to know that I cannot accomplish anything worthwhile without You. I long to accept weakness as a gift, knowing that Holy Spirit power consecrates my weakness. Give me courage Lord to lay down my Isaac on the altar and submit to Your will in every area of my life, knowing that divine plans are far superior to my own. You remain my shield and my heart trusts fully in You; it is then I am helped. My heart exalts You and may every morning song be filled with thanksgiving. You are so close to me when I am broken-hearted Lord, and my every thought is known by You before I speak. There is nothing You do not know about me: my past, my present, and my future. Such knowledge causes me to cling tightly to Your hand and trust You all the more. When I am crushed in spirit over my children, spouse, family, friends or other things in this world, I know that You are saving me from so great a destruction. You came to earth to destroy the works of the enemy in my life. There is no care or concern of mine that You are not intimately acquainted. You do not just want good in my life as I may see it with the natural eye, but you want 'the good' that conforms me to the image of Your Son. This may come through hardships, grief, pains, sorrows, joys, experiences, or daily diligence. It is in my weakness that Your consecrated glory shines through me. If others see any excellence in me, it is only a glimmer of who You Lord really are, and a bit of all that You want to be within me. For to me to live is Christ! You alone know the plans for my life. You alone wish to prosper me. You alone are true and give me a hope and a future. Praise you Jehovah Uzzi, My Forever Strength. I will not be downcast for You are the lifter of my head.

> *"The LORD bless you and keep you; the LORD make his face shine upon you and be gracious to you; the LORD turn his face toward you and give you peace"* (Numb. 6:24-26).

Chapter VIII

Esh Oklah, My Consuming Fire, *You are truly my breath and life alone. I will not be disheartened or let the disillusionment of the battle get the better of me, but I will continually rise up in Your joy and Your power for You **Jehovah Mekaddishkem are the Lord Who Sanctifies Me**. What lies ahead is far greater than I could ever imagine. I know what You have in store for me is magnificent and I will not fear the supernatural. I come Lord, I come!*

"For the Lord your God is a consuming fire (Esh Oklah), a jealous God"
(Deut. 4:24).

Winter's Fire

Frosted windows, scattered shadow of the pine
Sunbeams pierce the gray of day
The whisper of your Voice is mine
Calling me to linger, Come stay

Fire blazing, worship songs resound
Peace complete, amid a world of sin
Your nearness and grace abound
Telling me again, my Victor, we win!

Could time of moments, days, and years be shed
As fragmented light that shines so bright
Around me as a cloak of divinity spread
For Your Spirit is life, truth, complete sight

I praise Jesus for this freedom given
Consuming me as the fire I see
Faithful friend and Savior, no longer driven
The Great I AM telling me who to be

As we learned in chapter six how certain seeds do not germinate until they have been touched by fire's flames, the Christian's faith and character too are brought to maturity through life's trials. Just as human seed produces life, God's divine seed immediately began to produce the life of God inside you the moment you believed Jesus is the Son of God. It produced life in you because Jesus died for your sins, and rose on the third day destroying sin, death and the grave.

There is a story that a very distinguished botanist, who was exiled from his native land, obtained great insight as he worked as a gardener. On one occasion his employer received a valuable plant but was unfamiliar with its nature and needs. When he placed it in the hothouse under the glare of the sun, it soon began to wilt. It appeared to be dying. So the new gardener was asked to examine it. Quickly identifying its origin, he explained that this particular plant was an arctic plant, which cannot thrive in tropical heat. He immediately took it outside and exposed it to the frost, heaping pieces of ice around the flowerpot. Before long it became healthy and flourished again. Christian character is developed in many ways. The patterns of that process differ from one believer to the next. There is no formula for how God chooses to form and fashion our lives. He is the potter and we the clay. He simply asks us to trust Him and the manual He's given us in the Word.

The following testimony is shared for God's glory alone!

Ezekiel 43:5 says, *"So the Spirit took me up, and brought me into the inner court, and behold, the glory of the Lord filled the house."*

There is a time for every purpose under heaven. On November 14, 2009 I was praying for discernment in knowing how and when to tell others all that happened that weekend at a Women's Conference I had attended. God was infusing humility with my royal heritage, seemingly in opposition to one another, and knitting them together in my spirit. Knowing humility in the flesh is one thing, but experiencing it before a holy God in the spirit is quite another. Fear of God in reverence allows us, by His power, to then stand in the robes of Jesus' righteousness and know both our inheritance and our call. The Lord allowed me to expe-rience this truth in a profound way that weekend. I have only shared this with a few close sisters in Christ and my family, but believe I am to now share it here for the encouragement of others. I boast only in Jesus Christ and what He did in and through me that day; so that Father God, Jesus, and Holy Spirit might be glorified in its telling.

Journal Entry dated Nov. 14, 2009: Praise You Lord! Thank you for using this unworthy vessel in power and might. Never in my wildest imaginings would I have considered the day I just had. Thank You! Your presence was so strong in that place, so consuming in my being, so electrifying I can scarce put in words the experience. Let me try for future generations who may be blessed by the telling. You Holy Spirit are real and mighty! I serve a mighty God and Christ's resurrection power exists in His people because His Spirit exists in us.

Yesterday I came to a women's conference with an expectant heart and two dear friends, Barb and Pauline, came with me. The worship was sweet and the speakers blessed my heart as they brought forth the Word. They were the same messages that you Lord had planted in my own heart to deliver at a recent women's night at our church. It was on our royal inheritance, the authority of Christ, and our radiance as the Bride of Christ. These speakers were speaking on the exact same things. Through every speaker You were confirming in my heart Your presence, faithfulness, love, and sweet guidance.

The morning message was on Hab. 1:5 and Hab. 3:2.

> *Look at the nations and watch—and be utterly amazed.*
> *For I am going to do something in your days that you*
> *would not believe, even if you were told* (Hab. 1:5).

> *LORD, I have heard of your fame; I stand in awe of your*
> *deeds, LORD. Repeat them in our day, in our time make*
> *them known; in wrath remember mercy* (Hab. 3:2).

Lord, I do stand in awe and sing a new song as I dance before Your throne for all You have done this day! Where to start? After the message on being radiant, women were called forward to receive more of the Holy Spirit in their lives. Though I had received the baptism in the Holy Spirit at seventeen and experienced multiple infillings since then, I always long for more. I did not go up when the leaders were called up to pray for others even though I was on the prayer team. I went up for prayer because I tend to be a 'leaky vessel'. I wanted to receive a fresh touch. I was glued to my seat at that point. I truly sensed God wanted me to receive more, so instead of praying for others I felt I was to accept prayer.

I went to a dear friend, Stephanie, for prayer and we prayed for one another. I stepped back afterwards, and I noticed the aisles were so packed full of ladies that I could not return to my seat. Since I could hardly move one way or the other, I stayed at the altar and worshipped God. At one point I felt the Lord speaking to me to pray for the women, so I opened my eyes and saw the lines for prayer at the front. I, however, did not feel led to join the leaders up front at this point since I had not gone forward initially. I felt the Lord saying, "Turn Around!" As I turned around I felt a physical cloak laid on my shoulders. I knew it was a mantle of Christ's Righteousness; His presence palatable as I saw the hundreds of women standing in the aisles. Christ's compassion flooded my soul. I heard, "Pray for these my daughters." I first stood in place with my hands upheld and began praying over the crowd. I then felt the Spirit tell me to, "Go among them." I then stepped out and started praying; at that first step I was flooded with wave after wave of liquid love, power, energy, compassion. It was a consuming fire pouring forth through me. I could not contain the power or fire within. It was as though the floodgates of heaven were rushing through my spirit. I was laying hands on the women and declaring the righteousness of Christ in their lives and Holy Spirit fell on each one. Ladies started to be baptized in the Spirit and were slain before me. I continued down the aisle praying, declaring all God had for His daughters: healing, deliverance, and restored relationships, whatever the Spirit filled my mouth with. The Lord spoke revelatory truth to me about bondages, health issues, and other things and chains in the spirit realm fell crashing around us. From the front to the back women were slain in the Spirit. I believed I was walking into the palaces of His Kingdom here on the earth. When I got to the end of the large conference area, I turned around and most of the women in the center aisle had been slain in the Spirit. I laid on my face and praised God for using me in such a way. I heard "Get up, I'm not finished!" so I got up and continued down a few other aisles praying for women and the power of God still met needs in the crowd. I was awestruck.

I took off the Jesus scarf I was wearing and waved it in honor and benediction to my King Jesus. As I attempted to return to where I was standing next to Pauline, a woman came up to me. Her name was Sarah. She was an older woman, and she prophesied over me for close to 10 minutes. I prayed that God would allow me the privilege to remember as much of that prophesy as I could.

Be honored in the telling Lord:

Earlier in this weekend we threw in the trash anything that was holding us captive or in bondage. I had written "Broken Dreams". Sarah used those exact words in her prophecy.

The Lord says…"I have chosen you from before you were born. I have chosen you, a holy vessel to preach my Word and bring restoration to others. I will take your broken dreams, pain, tears, and sorrow and I will do a new thing. I have called you to serve my people. I have placed upon you a robe of royal inheritance; step into your inheritance and destiny in my Kingdom. I will bind up the pain and heal your marriage, I will heal your children's lives and bring them back, I will restore to you lost dreams, broken promises, and long awaited hopes. I have anointed you and called you. You are forever mine. Trust me, be in the Word, and search for hidden treasures. I am with you.

Alleluia Lord! Exhaustion overwhelmed me but I am so in awe of Who God is!

That is what my memory recalled but she had spoken for quite a while. The Lord dropped "Designing Treasures" into my spirit for an upcoming event I was planning and I was so excited about all that He would do. So as that conference ended I decided to stay one more night alone in the hotel just to be with the Lord. I read from Hebrews 6-9.

Read Hebrews 6:6-19.

How much more, then, will the blood of Christ, who
through the eternal Spirit offered himself unblemished to

God, cleanse our consciences from acts that lead to death, so that we may serve the living God (Heb. 9:14).

10:08 PM *"The fruit of the Spirit is love, joy, peace, long-suffering, kindness, goodness, faithfulness, gentleness, and self-control"* (Gal. 5:22-23).

The following prophetic excerpt was taken from my journal in 2009 at this same conference that night. I believe this word is still true over myself and over those who read it. Our circumstances may change, our world may spin out of control, but God never changes, and He wants to celebrate life with us through all eternity. I believe this word is for all of us for such a time as this!

Rhema Word:

You will bear fruit for My kingdom, not of yourself, but by My power. I will keep you at My feet and in My presence. You are forever Mine. Tell them to wage war against the enemy and stand firm in their faith. Show them they must claim my promises in full and not in part. Obey My voice as you hear the call in the moments of your life. I am restoring you to full measure. The mantle you felt me place on you today is yours. Wear it boldly. I know your heart is ever Mine. I have built you up to walk royally. Let no pride or arrogance be yours in this age. All glory must be mine. All honor must be mine. Be careful how you walk. Be careful how you speak. Discern spirits, divide marrow with my sword of truth. Understand and rejoice in sufferings and learn from them. Take authority over all things as I direct you. Claim freedom over lives and watch what I will do. Be obedient in all things, even when I stir your spirit at night and say, "Get up!" My people must get up not only from their rest, but also from their complacency and apathy. Get up and do kingdom work. Get up and listen to My voice. Get up!

1:45 AM – I saw the Savior's hands cupped, holding a dove. He released the dove to me, out of the wounds of His hands and said, "From death, unto life!" Praise God!

Take all that is dead in me Lord and bring it to newness of life.

> *They feast on abundance of your house, you give them drink from your river of delight* (Ps. 36:8).–AMEN!

> *The secret things belong to the Lord our God but the things 'revealed' belong to us and to our children forever, that we may follow all the words of the law* (Deut. 29:29).

LESSON 8
GET UP- I'm not finished!

Read Judges 6:1-7:25

The Israelites worshipped false gods and idols more than once, and the story of Gideon starts with the Lord being angry with them for falling yet again. The Lord left them, as a result, in the hands of the Mideanites for seven years. Finally they had had enough, and cried out to God for help and the Lord chose to send Gideon. This young man was threshing wheat and an angel appears before him, and told him the Lord was with him. The angel even called him a mighty warrior, a man of valor. He then tells Gideon that he will deliver the Israelites from the Midianites. Gideon asks for a sign and the angel of the Lord spontaneously combusts the food Gideon had brought him and realizes this angel is really from God.

That same night the angel tells Gideon to destroy one of the idol altars honoring Baal, and replace it with an altar to God and sacrifice a bull on it. Gideon does so at night so as not to be caught by the people. The townspeople discover it was Gideon and demand his execution but Joash, his father, said if Baal was truly god he could defend himself.

Gideon then calls others to come alongside him to fight against the Midianites. As you read the rest of the story answer a few of the following questions:

1. What sign did Gideon ask for to know God was with them?

2. God asked Gideon to decrease the size of the army several times, why did God do this?

3. Judges 7:2 tells us the purpose of such a small army. What was it?

4. What was Gideon's dream and what did it foretell?

Lessons from Gideon:

Consider how Gideon learned to trust God step by step. If the angel told Gideon that he would only have 300 soldiers to defeat 135,000 he might have had a really hard time believing the message was from God. God led him through a process of belief. He does that with us too. Some believe Gideon was fearful, but I tend to think he was rather brave. No one else was out threshing wheat, talking to angelic beings, and tearing down altars with the Midianites nearby. Was Gideon's response to the angel fear or humility? Of course we cannot be sure, but I am sure many were probably hiding in their homes and possibly starving, while Gideon was actively doing something for the people. Think about the importance of actively responding to the faith within us.

I loved hearing all the stories of those who kept going out of their homes during COVID scares to help others. God's mandates do not stop to be true, nor do his commands change just because the land is in an uproar and there is a plague in the land. He continues to speak to his people. The question remains however, do his people hear his voice?

In Judges 6:14 the angel told Gideon he would save Israel, and he responded by asking if God was for Israel where was He now. That in itself is a pretty courageous question, or perhaps naïve given his youth. Gideon knew the Scriptures and the power of God. He knew that God could do what He said.

Read these portions of Scripture again and write out what thoughts you have, or what impacts you the most in each section. Be ready to discus with your small group.

Altar of Baal (Judges 6:25-32)-

Gideon's Fleece (Judges 6:36-40)-

Too Many Men (Judges 7:2-8)-

An Encouraging Dream (Judges 7:9-14)-

Victory (Judges 7:15-23-8:3)-

5. What comforts or perceived securities would you have to abandon to fully obey God?

6. God called Gideon in the midst of an everyday task. How can God use a daily task in your life in his calling for you?

7. What area of your life do you think God wants you to concentrate on at this time?

8. Why do you think it is critical for believers to understand their identity before moving forward into their destiny?

Final thoughts from the Word to consider and meditate on:

> *To the weak I became weak, to win the weak. I have become all things to all people so that by all possible means I might save some (I Cor. 9:22).*

> *For I resolved to know nothing while I was with you except Jesus Christ and him crucified (I Cor. 2:2).*

You did not choose me, but I chose you and appointed you so that you might go and bear fruit, fruit that will last, and so that whatever you ask in my name the Father will give you (John 15:16).

Therefore go and make disciples of all nations, baptizing them in the name of the Father and of the Son and of the Holy Spirit (Matt. 28:19).

LESSON 8 B- FRUITFULNESS

What fruit am I producing? (Bearing Fruit for His Purpose with an aroma of His Love)

Read Proverbs 31: 25-31.

The oldest living things on earth are the bristlecone pines in the Ancient Bristlecone Pine Forest in the White Mountains of California and the Great Basin National Park in Nevada. They have endured for 4,800 years. The oldest dates from 2900 B.C. These trees were growing when Moses was given the Ten Commandments on Mount Sinai. They were already ancient when Christ was on earth. Remarkable they still produce seeds that germinate and grow. But men's spirits will live longer than any of these. Eventually the bristlecone pines will die, but the human soul was made for eternity.

The fruit of the righteous is a tree of life, and he who wins souls is wise (Prov. 11:30).

Remember this — a farmer who plants only a few seeds will get a small crop. But the one who plants generously will get a generous crop (2 Cor. 9:6)

And those who are peacemakers will plant seeds of peace and reap a harvest of goodness (James 3:8).

But those who drink the water I give will never be thirsty again. It becomes a fresh, bubbling spring within them, giving them eternal life (John 4:14).

Multitudes, multitudes in the valley of decision! For the day of the Lord is near in the valley of decision. The sun and the moon will be darkened, and the stars no longer shine. The Lord will roar from Zion and thunder from Jerusalem; the earth and the sky will tremble. But the Lord will be a refuge for His people (Joel 3: 14-16).

What fruit do we bear for the kingdom of God?

LESSONS IN THE BLACKBERRY PATCH

I grew up in the outskirts of Pittsburgh, on old farmland turned development, in the 1950's. My Dad worked in the steel mills of Pittsburgh, and sometimes worked three jobs. Our home was a haven of rest from his troubled upbringing, and family was so very important to him. Raised by a grandmother and alcoholic father after his mother abandoned him as an infant, he did not even know he had a brother, who had been sent to live with an aunt. He discovered his brother in his twenties when he found a birth certificate at the records office and they eventually met. Our home was built of brick and weathered many storms. My three brothers and I would play in the fields surrounding our home for hours on end. We would play in the creek, explore abandoned caves, ride bikes, catch fireflies and build treehouses. Next door to our property was a blackberry patch. My older brothers, Ed and Mark, would take sickles and carve tunnels in the underbrush. My younger brother John and I would take buckets in there and collect the blackberries to bring home for our Mom to bake blackberry pies; the best in the world! Some people learn everything they need to know in kindergarten, but since the blackberry patch was my only kindergarten, I think I learned a lot right there about life. Let me share....

1. Be careful where you step.

Order my steps in your word: and let not any iniquity have dominion over me (Ps. 119:133).

If you were not careful where you walked in the blackberry patch, you might find your shoe stuck in the mud, your ankle entwined with thorny stems, or your hair tangled in the brambles. Life's like that! Have you ever found yourself attempting to find fruit in your life, and you just feel stuck? Life tends to take us on some thorny paths and if we are not careful, we will remain lost.

The steps of a good man are ordered by the LORD: and he delights in his way (Ps. 37:23).

I do not know about you, but I would like the Lord to delight in my ways. Too often, we get stuck in the mire of life, the routines and responsibilities, and our souls tend to be malnourished. We have no fruit in our lives, because we either detached from the vine, Jesus, or have stopped diligently pursuing a holy God.

Look up a few, or all, of the following Scriptures and write the truth you see in them or ask the Lord a question if there's something you do not understand. Remember, the Lord does not mind the tough questions; we sometimes believe wrongly that He either does not care or will not take the time to listen.

- 1 Sam. 3:9
- Ps. 7:9

- Ps. 18:19
- Ps. 37:31
- Ps. 40:2
- Ps. 41:11
- Ps. 66:9
- Ps. 90:17
- Ps. 119:5
- Ps. 147:11
- Prov. 16:9
- Ps. 17:5
- Ps. 85:13
- Ps. 121:3
- Ps. 4:26

After reading the above Scriptures and meditating on them share a time when you felt stuck.

How has God brought you through?

2. Once the harvest is ready, fruit is evident on a daily basis!

> *Then he said to his disciples, "The harvest is plentiful but the workers are few* (Matt. 9:37).

Once the berries were ripe, they seemed to be filling the branches daily. We had to be out there every day picking berries, or the birds would claim the harvest. Daily due diligence is a good thing in earthly harvests and heavenly ones as well. Daily attention to our soul's needs is so critical. Are we feeding on daily manna in the word? The enemy lays claim to fruit in our lives in an attempt to destroy it both physically and spiritually. He comes to steal, kill and destroy much like those birds.

Meditate on these Scriptures: Luke 10:2; Matt. 13:39; Joel 1:11

Read about the Vine and the Branches in John 15:1-17. Pay special attention to verses 2, 4 and 16. I am sure the Lord will speak to us when we see him face to face. I wonder if Jesus will ask if I bore fruit in His name.

- From John 15, how are we told to bear fruit? By doing what?

3. Effort is needed to go to the garden each day

Effort and work are prominent themes in the Scriptures as they are in life, as seen in Matthew 9:37 where Jesus said to his disciples, "The harvest is plentiful but the workers are few". There are those in our culture who would have us believe that we should not put forth any effort, but simply rely on others. God never intended for us to be idle. He has gifts, dreams and work for us to do. Peter wrote in 2 Peter 1:15, *"And I will make every effort to see that after my departure, you will always be able to remember these things."*

- Who was making an effort here?

- Who is the audience in this passage?

- What things did he want them to remember? (Read verses before this verse.)

In 2 Peter 3:14 we read, *"So then, dear friends, since you are looking forward to this, make every effort to be found spotless, blameless and at peace with him."*

- What were they looking forward to? (Read surrounding Scriptures.)

- What can we do to be found spotless when Christ returns?

In Heb. 4:11 it states, *"Let us, therefore, make every effort to enter that rest, so that no one will perish by following their example of disobedience."*

- What rest is this passage speaking of? (Read surrounding Scriptures.)

2 Peter 1:10 states, *"Therefore, my brothers and sisters, make every effort to confirm your calling and election. For if you do these things, you will never stumble."*

- How can we 'confirm' our calling?

- Why should we confirm our calling?

Read the following Scriptures prayerfully and come to terms in your own spirit the differences you see. You will need to go out to the surrounding Scriptures to determine true meaning.

Rom. 9:16, *It does not, therefore, depend on human desire or effort, but on God's mercy. ... So then it does not depend on human will or effort but on God who shows mercy. ...*

Eph. 4:3, *Make every effort to keep the unity of the Spirit through the bond of peace. ... making every effort to keep the unity of the Spirit in the bond of peace. ...*

Luke 13:24, *"Make every effort to enter through the narrow door, because many, I tell you, will try to enter and will not be able to. ...*

Heb. 12:14, *Make every effort to live in peace with everyone and to be holy; without holiness no one will see the Lord. ...*

Rom 14:19, *Let us therefore make every effort to do what leads to peace and to mutual edification. ...*

- How do you reconcile some of these Scriptures like Rom. 9:16 (read that text in context) in knowing when to make an effort and when to trust in God's provision and will?

- What types of things are we told to make an effort in?

- We often think of '**walking** in the garden' with the Father in our private time. How does '**working** in the garden' change our idea about being in the garden daily?

4. <u>Making paths between the thorny bushes is necessary.</u>

Paul had a thorn in his flesh that theologians still debate as to the root. Whether it was his eyesight from the blindness at his conversion or some other ailment, Paul did not give up and he fulfilled the call of God on his life. He sought no excuses and gave no complaints, he trusted God and kept the great commission of preaching the Word in season and out. We too will experience thorns in this life, whether they are circumstances, illnesses, infirmities, people, or our own hang-ups, but God is able to move us past them for His glory and His purpose. He can turn our battle scars into beauty marks, our ashes into crowns. *"There are those who rebel against the light, who do not know its ways or stay in its paths"* (Job 24:13). Let us not be numbered among them.

Read these Scriptures and answer the following questions: Ps. 25:4; Ps. 23:3; Prov. 3:6.

- What Godly characteristics do you see in these verses?

- What should be our ultimate purpose in learning and following the Lord's paths?

- What are some thorns in your own life that get in the way of serving God?

Read these Scriptures and answer the following questions: Ps. 57:2; Prov. 15:19; Luke 6:44; Joshua 23:13.

- Identify some thorns in your life that keep you from bearing fruit and yielding a harvest for the Kingdom.

- What does bearing fruit mean to you?

"They arrayed Him in crimson, placed on His head a wreath of thorny twigs which they had twisted" (Mark 15:17). We can yield all the thorns in our life to the one who bore a crown of thorns on His head to set us all free. Jesus wore the thorns on His head, bleeding out from His brow, so that we can be redeemed. Are you able to place your 'thorns' from the questions above on our Savior and trust Him to bring a harvest in and through your life? He longs to give us His own mind. Some of us have not surrendered our 'thorns' in this world to our Savior, and instead hide behind them as excuses for disobedience, complacency or outright rebellion against God. We play the blame game and blame God for the things we think should be different in our lives. We blame others for our own sins and failures. If we would concentrate on thanking God for all the good He has showered on us instead of focusing all our attention on the lack or suffering in our life, perhaps then He will be able to use us to bear more fruit in the Kingdom.

When the Israelites saw they were in trouble because the army was hard-pressed, they hid in caves, in thorny thickets, among rocks, in pits, and in cisterns (1 Sam. 13:6). Read Chapter 13 in 1 Samuel to gain perspective in this verse.

- Do we sometimes hide in our thorny thickets when we are hard-pressed, because we never trusted Christ with them?

- Let us identify our real fears of the enemy that keep us in hiding; the fears that keep us from fulfilling God's call on our life. List them here then look for an opposing verse to claim and decree over yourself as you begin to walk in victory.

Let me give you some examples; you can even choose from this list:

- If I think something is impossible, I can claim Luke 18:27.
- If I think I cannot forgive someone, I can claim 1 John 1:9 and Romans 8:1.
- If I think I am too tired to obey God, I can claim Matthew 11:28-30.
- If I think I cannot figure things out, I can claim Proverbs 3:5-6.
- If I am experiencing fear, I can claim 2 Timothy 1:7.
- If I am experiencing worry and frustration, I can claim 1 Peter 5:7.
- If I feel all alone, I can claim Hebrew 13:5.
- If I am overwhelmed by life, I can claim Philippians 4:19.
- If I think I cannot do something, I can claim Philippians 4:13.
- If I feel as though I cannot go on, I can claim 2 Corinthians 12:9 and Psalm 91:15.
- If I believe the lie that nobody loves me, I can claim John 3:16 and John 3:34.

If you are already walking in victory, Praise God! Perhaps you can think of a friend who may need mentoring or encouragement in one of these areas. God can use each of us to plant seeds in someone else's life, as He helps us take the focus off ourselves.

5. Sometimes the fruit is hidden behind the leaves-Hidden Treasures.

I love to think of hidden treasures. Sometimes as I looked for those blackberries there were hidden surprises in those woods. I would at times trip over an old farm tool, and other times I would find a little bunny nest or forgotten toy. As a child my joy overflowed. Our joy too can overflow as we find the hidden truths of God's Word. One way to study Scripture is to do a word study and try to pull out what God is saying. Let's do a word study on 'hidden treasures'. Dig in and find the treasures; record your thoughts:

Isa. 45:3 -
I Cor. 2:7 -
Obadiah 1:6 -
I Cor. 4:5 -
Matt. 13:35 -
Job 28:21 –

- What is Job referring to as being hidden here in Job 28:21?

- Share with your group something you learned after reading these Scriptures.

Read: Col. 2:3; Mark 4:22.

- As you read these Scriptures how did the Lord speak to your heart?

- Why does God hide things from His people? What do you think His motivation is?

My eyes are on all their ways; they are not hidden from me, nor is their sin concealed from my eyes (Jer. 16:17).

- God has hidden things from us, but we cannot hide things from God. How can understanding this thought transform our own thinking?

- What should be our position before God if we wish to receive the hidden treasures of His kingdom?

6. **Some of the fruit is rotten because it was not picked on time.**

I love how the Lord uses nature to teach us spiritual truths. As the blackberries lingered too long on the vine because I was too lazy to get up, so too fruit not picked in due season withers and dies. Souls are dying and the harvest is plentiful but the workers are few. Let it not be said of us that we did not work in the fields, or that we did not get up; some will plant, some will water, and some will yield the increase. May souls not be lost because of our disobedience. May souls not rot on the vine, because we chose the mixture of this world in our lives. We must stay connected to our vine, Jesus Christ, as we read in John 15.

Record these two Scripture:

Luke 6:43

- Have you ever refused to obey the Lord and later regretted a missed opportunity to witness to someone or show a kindness?

- The Lord certainly shows us mercy, but how important do you think it is to obey the Lord immediately?

If we are walking in fellowship with Holy Spirit, we have the mind of Christ. Sometimes we delay in decision making because we really want time to disobey or forget about something the Lord is prompting us to do. Are we discerning His voice in the moments and asking for Holy Spirit guidance and wisdom, or do we too often say, "I'll pray about it?" or, "I'll do it later?" Prayerfully consider this question.

7. <u>The red juice stains our hands.</u>

Stained hands on a child coming out of the blackberry patch were common. Stained hands now hold greater consequences in my spirit. Physical stains were easily washed away, but the stain of sin is removed only by my Savior. Spiritual stains are washed away as we repent and come before God; confessing our sins, believing in Jesus, trusting and following Him as our Lord and Savior, completely surrendered to His will and ways. This is a continual walk in the garden with Abba Father, Jesus and Holy Spirit. We are to tell them all about our failures, triumphs, thoughts, desires, joys, sorrows, pains and ambitions. Our God wants to hear about it all.

Write our these Scriptures and comment on what God is speaking to you:

Isaiah 59:3

Job 31:7

Psalm 7:3

Hebrews 9:14

Romans 5:9

Romans 3:25

Revelation 1:5

Hebrews 10:19

Colossians 1:20

We have all known the stain of sin on our hands. Sometimes when we work in the garden of this world we can pick up stain, even in the act of serving and reaping a harvest. Keeping our hands and hearts clean before a holy God is a daily act of our will. We have to learn the power associated with the blood of Jesus. Taking communion and pleading the blood of Jesus over our lives will bring victory, and greater union with Abba Father. The Israelites spread the blood of a lamb over their doorposts so the angel of death would pass by in Egypt when Pharaoh's heart was hardened, and Moses called down plagues on the people. We too must know the power of the Lamb of God, Jesus Christ and his precious blood poured out on Calvary for each one of us. His Blood cancelled the debt of sin I owed a Holy God, and heals me from both my sin and sickness.

I declare and decree Scripture over my life every time the enemy attempts to put sickness or disease upon me. My husband and I have experienced multiple healings by praying Scriptures over our lives. We have witnessed many miracles of how God heals individuals from mental illness, addictions, infirmities and emotional trauma. I had sent healing Scriptures to a family in Pittsburgh recently whose father lay unconscious with a breathing tube from fourth stage cancer presumably, with little hope from the doctors for survival. I got a text several days ago that he woke up and was talking to his fifteen year old son on the phone. This morning, as I write this, I got another text from my friend that read:

"I wanted to give you another update on Don. He walked today with the assistance of PT and a walker. He was also started on a clear diet. To say this is wonderful is nothing short of a miracle. They have been able to diagnose his condition as autoimmune encephalitis. They have been treating him for the last 72 hours and he has made remarkable progress. Even his oncologist told his wife that he is a miracle. I wanted to pass this along because I believe the prayers have made all the difference and so does Don and his wife. I thought you would like to hear some good news given the state of our crazy world. (Second week of Russian/Ukraine War). Thanks so much for your prayers."

My God still heals and Jesus' blood still matters!

- What wrong type of stain can we get on our hands while harvesting in the fields of the kingdom here on this earth?

- Do your own study on the blood of Jesus. Share something you learned.

8. After picking the fruit remember to cleanse yourself.

After picking berries in that blackberry patch I usually needed to wash off. That physical cleansing was necessary to get rid of dirt, blackberry juice, and even ticks. Sometimes when we are out ministering we need to cleanse ourselves spiritually. In the course of doing the Lord's work, we can pick up some spiritual debris that tries to cling to us. It is so important to be in the Word, in the Lord's presence, and in prayer on a daily basis and discern when there is excess junk in our life. Staying pure before God is both Holy Spirit's assignment over us, and our own yielding to Holy Spirit, being aware of the spiritual battles we all face.

Read and record:

1 Peter 1:2

1 John 1:7

2 Tim. 2:21

If we keep ourselves pure, as He who dwells within us is pure, we will be a special vessel for honorable use.

- What are some ways we can keep ourselves pure

- What is the difference between being cleansed by God and cleansing ourselves?

Read and record:
Ezekiel 24:13

Isaiah 1:16

• What is our role in staying pure before God?

• What is God's role?

9. <u>The garden is a peaceful place.</u>

Some of my sweetest childhood memories are picking berries or wading in the creek. Sometimes I would hide from my brothers in the rambling pathways, and just listen to the song of a blue jay or watch a butterfly flit on a leaf. Peace comes to mind when I remember those blissful days. God's garden too is full of his beauty, His presence and His peace. It is both a restful and sublime place as well as a work place. My greatest joys as an adult have been in service to my King. As a young Christian, I thought much of the peace of personal spiritual nourishment in the garden, but I really did not much consider the work that needed to be done. It is like the child watching their father in the garden; enjoying the father's companionship, but not contributing to the work at hand. As one matures, they are expected to help and be about their father's business. Now I realize Jesus refreshes us beside still waters, so we will then turn and tell others of His garden. Some of my greatest joys now are interceding for others, speaking to women about Christ in the prison, mentoring new believers, sharing a Bible study time, or worshipping before the Lord. I find indescribable peace in serving. We are all to be about our Abba Father's work.

Gardens are one of those themes in Scripture that take us from the Garden of Eden to the Garden Tomb (John 19:41), and then to the gardens that must exist in heaven. In the Song of Solomon 4:16 we read, *"Blow on my garden, that its fragrance may spread everywhere. Let my beloved come into his garden and taste its choice fruits."* That is what it is like to experience the love of Jesus as his Spirit comes like a gently blown wind, and we experience the fragrance of His presence. I actually experienced the sweet fragrance of Christ several times in worship or prayer. May we taste of his choice fruit as we serve Him in the kingdom work He has for us.

- Your life is a garden and we need to die with Christ to live again. What needs to die in the garden of your life so you may live fully for Christ?

- Read Isa. 61:11. How does righteousness and praise spring up in someone's life? Is it springing up in your life? If not, why not? If so, how so?

#8. Another obstacle that keeps us from enjoying a right relationship with the Father as his sons or daughter is fear of the supernatural. I know for myself I have sometimes needed to step back from things I saw or heard because they were outside my comfort zone. Believe me when I tell you, the experience I opened this chapter with was never even considered as a possibility in my life, yet it happened just as I described. Many Christians are not comfortable when they hear others speaking in tongues, speaking prophetically, or telling of dreams and visions. Being slain in the Spirit is not worded as such in the Bible, but many 'fell on their face as dead' when encountering angelic beings or God's Spirit. All these things are in the Bible, and they were not just for a time or season, for our God changes not. He still speaks to his people in dreams and visions. He still uses tongues and interpretation to encourage His church. I heard of a man who was compelled to speak in tongues on an airplane, he obeyed, and the man next to him was saved because he was declaring the gospel in that man's native tongue. The kingdom of our God and King cannot be fully understood, that is why the Lord tells us to not lean on our own understanding, but in all our ways to acknowledge Him. If we are seeking God with our whole heart, mind and soul, we should expect our very nature to be infused with his presence, a truly new creation. The result will be lasting fruit in the kingdom of God.

A PRAYER TO ESH OKLAH, MY CONSUMING FIRE

Esh Oklah, My Consuming Fire, you are truly my breath and life alone. I will not be disheartened or let the disillusionment of the battle get the better of me, but I will continually rise up in joy and power for You Jehovah Mekaddishkem are the Lord Who Sanctifies Me. I will not fear the ways of Your kingdom or supernatural living for they are my life and destiny. I praise You as You burn me holy for Your divine purposes on the earth. I declare and decree that I am being purified by your Spirit. I declare and decree that I will pursue Your presence daily and listen to Your voice. I declare and decree that You are purging the dross from my life as I partner in obedience to Your call. I declare that signs, wonders and miracles will follow me all the days of my life, because I am your child, born of Your nature and Your love. I declare and decree that I will stand up in boldness and courage in the face of opposition, and I will not fall back. I pray this in Jesus' name.

Chapter IX

Garden of Gethsemane

*Forgive me Lord when I think it is about my own righteousness, because apart from you, I have none. Impart to me all that I need of your righteousness alone, to face yet another journey, yet another giant. I know I am precious to You **Jehovah Tsidkenu, My Righteousness,** and that You love me so very much; as I do You.*

> *In His days Judah will be saved, and Israel will dwell securely. And this is His name by which He will be called. "The LORD our righteousness* (Jehovah Tsidkenu) (Jer. 23:6).*

LET ME HEAR

Let me hear the angels sing
Oh, let me hear their praise
Let me touch the hem of God
One worship from our souls to raise

Let me know Your Word of Truth
Oh, to see your precious face
Let me kneel before your throne
In me create your love and grace

Let me hear the angels sing
Oh, change me in your sight
Let me stand within your courts
As you meet me through each night

Let me know the inner courts
That day I tell my story
Let me sing anew with them
The angels' song of glory

Let me hear the rush of wings
As angels resound your glory
Let the work you had given me
Forever tell your story

*So the Spirit took me up, and brought me into the inner
court, and behold, the glory of the Lord filled the house*
(Ezekiel 43:5).

He will be called. "The LORD our righteousness (Jehovah Tsidkenu)."
but what righteousness do we display as we are being formed into his

image? Scripture tells us that our own righteousness is as filthy rags. What lies at the core of our spirituality that gives purpose, meaning and direction to all we do? Are we examples of godly living and is God's presence sensed in all we do? Giving attention to the nature of the meaning of the presence of God in our life and his righteousness is what we will explore in this lesson.

All throughout Scripture we see examples of leaders who had a profound sense of living in the presence of God. In the Old Testament, Moses, as he led the Israelites to the Promised Land, begged God, *"If your Presence does not go with us, do not send us up from here. How will anyone know that you are pleased with me and with your people unless you go with us?"* (Exodus 33:15). The word 'presence' here from the Hebrew word 'panim' means 'face'. *"The Lord would speak to Moses face to face, as a man speaks with his friend"* (Exodus 33:11). What a vision of the nearness and intimacy of God that Moses had with Him, that even his own face shone. (See Exodus 34:29). In the New Testament one example is Paul in Corinth when he preached *"with a demonstration of the Spirit's power"* (1 Corinthians 2:4). Paul was ever aware of his own weaknesses and the thorn in his flesh, but he was also aware of the power within. (See 2 Corinthians 12:9). Moses and Paul were both yielded vessels and God's Presence and working in their lives was evident. Their passion to submit to God's working in and through them are examples for us today. They longed for the presence of God and we can to. Taste and see what God will do!

The Holy Spirit first enters our life at our confession of sin and faithful acceptance of Christ as Lord and Savior. Jesus taught Nicodemus, and us, that it is necessary to be "born again" by the work of the Holy Spirit: *"Flesh gives birth to flesh, but the Spirit gives birth to spirit"* (John 3:6). This regeneration of our spirit is the first call into the presence of God, and one that opens the way of communion with our heavenly Father. The anointing presence of God is often used in referring to those who pray, preach or teach with authority and empowering presence of the Holy Spirit, but we are all called to the anointing of Holy Spirit in our lives. We are to live victorious over our own brokenness first, and then reach out to others. Learning this has taken me 40 years. Lord willing it will not take you as long.

Read Titus 3:5. Research the Hebrew in this text. What did you discover?

Read I Peter 1:3. What hope is given?

Read 2 Corinthians 5:17. What are we now called?

LESSON 9
Trading My Image for His

All of us have been influenced by others trying to define us in a 'false-self' based on this world's standards, culture, and lies. No one escapes from developing a false self, and our language about the self reflects this. The very word *person* comes from Latin *per sonare* meaning to *sound through*. The idea is of a mask, through which an actor speaks. May the Lord Jesus tear down every mask, chain, and veil in our lives and allow each of us to truly see how much God actually loves us.

The purpose of our lives as Christians is to be conformed into Christ's image so that we may glorify Him in all we do.

- What thoughts, words or feelings come immediately to your mind when you think of yourself, your abilities, your accomplishments, your failures, and your sorrows?

- In the above question what did you tend to focus on? (Abilities or disabilities, joys or sorrows, accomplishments or failures).

What we answered to those questions was determined by experiences, lies from the enemy we have believed, as well as thoughts we and others have spoken over us for years. Our words hold the power of life and death. No matter what our pasts were like, how we see ourselves right now matters. Some tend to have more of a negative assessment, some more positive. In the end, we all need to be set free from the identity the world assigns us and align with the identity that our Creator assigns us. We all need to come through the righteousness and blood of Jesus on the cross. Some of us need to be humbled, some built up, but all of us need transformed by the power of Jesus and Holy Spirit. We need to align our mouths with the Word, our thoughts with his Spirit, and our opinion of ourselves with the opinion of our Creator. His books were written of our destinies long before we were even born.

Christ's cross is truly the expressed judgement of man's sin by a holy God. Jesus was not martyred, He willingly came for the express purpose of laying down His life for the sin of mankind. The violence of the cross did not *happen* to Christ, because this sacrifice was His purpose. His accomplishment on the cross cannot be compared with any other event in all eternity; it was pivotal in the cosmos. Through Christ, redemption came to mankind to enter into relationship with God the Father. Revelation 13:8 tells us that the slaying of the Lamb of God was purposed and written in the foundations of the world. We cannot separate the fact of God being *made manifest in the flesh* from his being *made sin for us.* (See 1 Tim. 3:16; 2 Cor. 5:21). The cross exemplifies the very nature of God, and is a gate through which all who choose can enter into oneness with a holy God. We come to salvation at the cross, linger and abide in the life and person of Jesus Christ, and enter into the rest of faith and trust.

So how do we understand how to abide in His presence? How do we understand how to worship Him and be cleansed by the Word? How do we understand how to make faith choices that influence lives? Basically, we understand by seeking Him daily as we read the Word, having the Spirit of God in us, and being regenerated daily in Christ.

We can miss God's purpose for our lives if Christ's character and passion are not more noticeable in our lives every day. Many times, we think **doing** more for the Lord will make us more Christ-like, but truly it is about **being** transformed by His power into His likeness, as we are abiding with Him.

David Wilkerson said it best: *"If I am not becoming noticeably more like Christ, then I have totally missed God's purpose for my life...Christ-likeness isn't about what I do for the Lord, but about how I'm being transformed into His likeness."*[14]

We need to learn to be complete in Christ, believe what God's Word says about who Christ is in us, and behold this God we serve in daily reverence in the Holy of Holies. We were created for God and His purposes. Our fulfillment in life will only come when we align ourselves with <u>His</u> design and <u>His</u> intentions. We do this by looking to Jesus, the author and finisher of our faith.

In Matthew 5:8, Jesus said, *"Blessed are the pure in heart, for they will see God."*

In Psalm 27:8, we read *"My heart says of You, Seek His face! Your face, Lord, I will seek."* Take a sacred gaze daily into the Word and into the face and character of Jesus, and you will be transformed into His image.

Jesus told us in Luke 24:49, *"To be clothed with power from on high."* The big idea is that God is love, we are His Holy of Holies, the abiding place of His precious Holy Spirit. We can trade the old nature reflection of imperfect love for His reflection of perfect love. First, know this about yourself: *"The Spirit of God has made you, the breadth of the Almighty gives your life"* (Job 33:4). Embracing the foundational truths of our Creator is crucial.

Paul wrote to the Corinthian church to address some problems they were having in a city of pagan worship and deceitful living. Specifically he was addressing concerns about where the people were placing their priorities. Today, I would like to challenge you regarding your own. In 1 Corinthians chapter 12, Paul was speaking about the church as one body with many parts, and all the parts were important to the operation of the church. The last verse in 1 Cor. 12:31b states *"I will show you a still more excellent way."* That introduced the "Love Chapter" in 1Corinthians13. If the way you have chosen is not giving you peace, not meeting your expectations, or not fulfilling your deepest need, try *a more excellent way.*

After reading those verses, what is God showing you personally?

How do you interpret a more excellent way?

In John 13:34, Jesus said, *"A new commandment I give you. Love one another as I have loved you, so you must love one another."* We stumble in that command, because we have not looked into the mirror of who we truly are in relation first to God and then to others. We have not allowed the light of Christ's love to permeate our being in His presence. As a result we are hindered in walking a victorious life. We remain focused on ourselves and our selfishness is an idol. Focusing on our own problems, needs, failures, insecurities, and regrets is actually one way the enemy of our souls can keep us from advancing the Kingdom of God. Shake us all loose Lord from debilitating patterns of viewing our God, others, and ourselves in anything less than the light of Your love.

Our main verse is from 1Corinthians 13:12 *"For now we see only a reflection as in a mirror; then we shall see face to face. Now I know in part; then I shall know fully, even as I am fully known."*

"Now we see a reflection as in a mirror" is the first phrase of 1 Corinthians 13:12. We see a poor reflection, a cloudy picture if you will. This is an illustration of imperfect love and knowledge. How much do you yearn for God? Psalm 84:2 says, *"My soul yearns, even faints, for the courts of the Lord, my heart and my flesh cry out for the living God."* Oh that our passion would be such as this! Jesus is the Word and as we look into this Word we will see Jesus! As we receive every Word of Truth from the Scriptures, we receive more of Jesus through faith. Let us not just receive and believe the Word, but act on every word and promise by faith.

Mirrors in ancient times were made from brass and gave a poor reflection. In Exodus 38:8 *"And he made the laver of brass, and the foot of it of brass, of the looking glasses of the women assembling, which assembled at the door of the tabernacle of the congregation."* The priests would cleanse themselves at the laver. The women had offered up jewelry and mirrors as an offering in the building of the temple courts. How wonderful for the women to offer a measure of their own vanity and appearance to be used by God in cleansing the priests. Think about that for a minute. How much of our own image have we really given up to Christ? Or do we simply add Jesus to what we 'want', to what we 'will', or to what we 'do'? Do we offer up a measure of our own appearance or the fullness of who we are, for God's cleansing in our surrender? Something to think about!

So how do we cleanse daily spiritually?

In Ephesians 5:26 it reads, *"That he might sanctify and cleanse it* (speaking of the Church) *with the washing of water by the Word!"* Beloved, we need to look into the mirror of God's Word, the true mirror which shows us our own thoughts, attitudes, reasoning, and withheld forgiveness. This daily cleansing in the Word of God shows us who we really are. A daily look into the Word of God is to keep us ever aware of our need to reflect on our motives and attitudes as we commune and serve a Holy God in His Love. Holy Spirit will mold us and fashion us for the Master's use and glory.

It is time, time to allow Jesus to mold us, to transform us and to let His reflection be what people see when they look at us. Each morning, as we prepare for the day ahead, we generally do not leave the house without looking into a mirror. The mirror enables us to see if there is anything out of place, and gives us an opportunity to correct what is wrong. So often we can get wrapped up in our own ways that we set aside the ways of the One whom we are called to be like, whose image we are called to bear. We need to look in the mirror of the Word daily! Jesus has the power to change the person in the mirror! Sometimes we are enamored by a toxic self; too many selfies, too much me culture, and too much self-focus; it is all basically selfishness. Becoming Christ focused and other focused takes some effort on our part, but once we make that effort we will be the happier for it.

"Then we shall see face to face" is the second phrase in 1 Corinthians 13:12. Let us consider Moses and how he was changed by being in the presence of a Holy God! What happened when Moses spoke face to face with God? The Israelites could not even look at him for his face shone like the sun and he had to wear a veil over his face. Now there is a reason to cover one's face! Should not something happen daily as we meet face to face with a holy God? Abiding more and more in His Word truly does change us. It changes our countenance, it changes our character, it changes our motives, and it changes our behavior.

> *But whenever anyone turns to the Lord, the veil is taken away. Now the Lord is the Spirit, and where the Spirit of the Lord is, there is freedom. And we all, who with unveiled faces contemplate the Lord's glory, are being transformed into his image with ever-increasing glory, which comes from the Lord, who is the Spirit (2 Cor. 3:16-18).*

> *"The God who made the world and everything in it is the Lord of heaven and earth and he does not live in temples built by human hands"* (Acts 17:24).

> *"Don't you know that you yourselves are God's temple"* (I Cor. 3:16).

> *"I will dwell IN them, and walk IN them; and I will be their God and they shall be my people"* (2 Cor. 6:16, emphasis mine).

Meeting with God face to face in prayer, Bible reading, and worship are times of wonderful intimacy. We can come with praise and confidence because Jesus intercedes for us as high priest with the Father. *"Therefore, brothers and sisters, since we have confidence to enter the Most Holy Place by the blood of Jesus, by a new and living way opened for us through the curtain, that is, his body, and since we have a great priest over the house of God, let us draw near to God with a sincere heart and with the full assurance that faith brings, having our hearts sprinkled to cleanse us from a guilty conscience and having our bodies washed with pure water. Let us hold unswervingly to the hope we profess, for he who promised is faithful. And let us consider how we may spur one another on toward love and good deeds"* (Heb. 10:19-24). Our entire lives can be an act of worship as we yield to the agenda of heaven, the song of the angels, and the fire of Holy Spirit within.

> *"Enter His gates with thanksgiving and his courts with praise; give thanks to Him and praise His name"* (Psalm 100:4).

> *"Let us then approach God's throne of grace with confidence, so that we may receive mercy and find grace to help us in our time of need"* (Heb. 4:16).

As a believers we are the temple of a holy God and the journey of your worth, identity, and purpose can only be realized in and through Jesus Christ. We are being changed from faith to faith, glory to glory, and life to life, in and through Jesus, as we yield to Holy Spirit.

"Now I know in part" is the third phrase in 1 Corinthians 13:12. The outer court of the tabernacle was where the altar of sacrifice and the bronze laver stood. The blood sacrifice was required on the altar for the sins of the people. Jesus willingly laid down His life as the ultimate sacrifice as our perfect Lamb; this event was foreshadowed by the lambs in the tabernacle offering. This is the exact point that calls us to faith in Jesus and relationship with the Father, because Jesus atoned for our sins. We now have access to approach a Holy God because Jesus' blood covers our sins. In Exodus 30:17-22 we can see *"For as in Adam, all die; even so in Christ, all shall be made alive."* And is 1 Corinthians 15:21-22 it says *"For since death came through a man, the resurrection of the dead comes also through a man. For as in Adam all die, so in Christ all will be made alive."*

Our new life in Christ is not based upon what we do; rather it is based on who is in us and what we allow Holy Spirit to accomplish through us. The 'part' of truth we know is what we are then asked to act on in faith and trust. The more truth revealed to us, the more we are able to live it out in faith. Although we are in-Christ, we still have a free-will of the flesh. We must learn and purpose in our heart to bow down on the inside, and let Jesus rule daily. Let us not be lukewarm in this divine romance God has initiated. It tells us in Rev. 3:16 *"So, because you are lukewarm—neither hot nor cold—I am about to spit you out of my mouth."* God forbid that when Jesus returns for those who are eagerly awaiting him, He finds us lukewarm. Being lukewarm is having a divided heart, divided passions, divided focus, and not being completely sold out to the passion of our Savior, namely lost souls.

That is why Jesus died and spilled His blood; let us not crucify Him a second time.

"Then I shall know fully even as I am fully known" is the fourth phrase is 1 Corinthians 13:12. As God's new temple, let us take a fresh look at our identity. First, ask yourself: to whom am I looking at to see who I am as an individual, now that the Spirit of God dwells in me? Who has assessed what my self-worth is? And who defines my self-image? The truth is, that many of us have taken into our hearts and continue to believe that we are in fact, exactly what others have defined us to be. Parents, a spouse, a boyfriend, girlfriend or others who have been closely associated with us during our lifetime are most likely those who have inadvertently defined us. It may be either positive or negative; it matters not really. Now is the time to lay all of that down at the cross, and call it forth as good as dead and buried in the death of Jesus. Then rise up in the risen Christ to receive the truth of who you really are as a new creation in Christ. Let us be perfectly clear, God as your Creator, is the only reliable source of accurate information about who you are, what you can do, and who you are to be. We need to erase the repetitive recordings and strongholds in our minds of negative and destructive self-talk, lying predictions, dead dreams, and self-deprivation many of us have let run rampant in our souls for years. It may even be a recording of praise, success, or accomplishments. It does not have to be negative. Pride can enter in and God opposes pride. We need to pursue holiness and righteousness with a passion and rigor as running a race and know who we belong to.

"The Lord knows those who are his" (2 Timothy 2:19). His thoughts toward you outnumber the grains of sand. He formed you in your mother's womb. He knows the number of hairs on your head. He knows all your days before one of them came to pass. Let's be clear: That thing you have done, God does not hate you for it! Those things done to you, God does not despise you for them. Guilt and shame are covered by the

Blood of the Lamb and need not come between you and God, or you and yourself. God desires a more intimate relationship with you than you can currently imagine or believe. Let us cultivate that relationship daily as we take it on faith. If you could see yourself the way God does, through the eyes of Jesus His precious Son, you would do whatever it takes to grow into your true and divine identity. You would see why Jesus thought it worth it to suffer and die on that cross to restore and reclaim you as His own. If Jesus paid such a high price, should we not prize this life we have been given? Should we not pursue the perfection of His image in us with our whole heart, mind and soul?

We do not need to overcome all our failures and human screw ups on our own. Just gaze into the mirror of Christ, the mirror of His Word, and know today that He calls you His beloved. He tells us to come as we are; He has no favorites. We have all sinned and fallen short of His glory, but He longs to restore that glory to us through salvation and sanctification.

We must remember that Holy Spirit is the One Who transforms us, it is not our work! In order to help us with the transformation into His image, Christ gave us His Holy Spirit. The Holy Spirit is the third person of the Trinity. He is our comforter, counselor, helper, supporter, advisor, advocate and ally.

> *"Praise be to the God and Father of our Lord Jesus Christ, who has blessed us in the heavenly realms with every spiritual blessing in Christ. For he chose us in him before the creation of the world to be holy and blameless in his sight. In love he predestined us for adoption to sonship through Jesus Christ, in accordance with his pleasure and will, to the praise of his glorious grace, which he has freely given us in the One he loves. In him we have redemption through his blood, the forgiveness of sins, in accordance with the riches of God's grace that he lavished on us. With all wisdom and understanding, he made known*

to us the mystery of his will according to his good pleasure, which he purposed in Christ, to be put into effect when the times reach their fulfillment—to bring unity to all things in heaven and on earth under Christ. In him we were also chosen, having been predestined according to the plan of him who works out everything in conformity with the purpose of his will, in order that we, who were the first to put our hope in Christ, might be for the praise of his glory. And you also were included in Christ when you heard the message of truth, the gospel of your salvation. When you believed, you were marked in him with a seal, the prom-ised Holy Spirit" (Eph. 1:3-13).

Write out these verses and comment on anything the Lord shows you:

Eph. 2:8

1 Cor. 12:4-6

2 Cor. 13:14

2 Cor. 1:22

2 Cor. 3:18

When we become believers, God's Spirit comes to indwell us as a pledge, a seal or a mark of ownership, indicating that we now belong to God. This Spirit, then, is the One that sets about conforming us into Christ's image. His job is to first make Christ's presence known to us, and then *through us* to others. You may be asking how we can possibly do this. Let's look to Jesus.

How did Jesus love His Father? He said and did only what He heard the Father saying.

How did Jesus love Himself? He knew who He was! Jesus asked his apostles at one point who did the people say that He was. Let's be clear, Jesus was not having an identity crisis! *"But what about you?" he asked Peter, "Who do you say I am?" Peter answered, "You are the Messiah"* (Mark 8:29). He asked his friends to see if they had a true reflection of who He was; he did not ask because He did not know Himself. Once we have a true reflection of who Jesus is, then we will be better prepared to have a true reflection of ourselves through His eyes. There is a completion in Christ that is eternal! Gaze into His face and see Who He really is today and He will reveal to you who you are in Him.

He said:

a. *"I am the Bread of Life"* (John 6:35).
   - Bread sustains life when one is hungry; physical verses spiritual.
   - Are you offering physical and spiritual bread to others?

b. *"I am the Light of the World"* (John 8:12).
   - Light illuminates darkness and brings clarity and true sight.
   - Are you bringing the light of Christ into your relationships?

c. *"I am the Door of the Sheep"* (John 10:7).
   - Doors access places yet unknown to us as well as places of comfort.
   - Are you providing access to new knowledge and comfort to others?

d. *"I am the Good Shepherd"* (John 10:11).
   - Shepherds lead and guide those who need direction.
   - Has Jesus guided you and are you guiding others toward Christ?

e. *"I am the resurrection and the Life"* (John 11:25).
   - Resurrection and Life from death and deception
   - Does your life exemplify life or death; truth or lies?

f. *"I am the true Vine"* (John 15:1-5).
- A vine brings life giving sap to bear fruit in abundance.
- Are you connected to this vine and bearing fruit for the Kingdom?

"Who when He was reviled did not revile in return" (1 Peter 2:23). When Jesus was tempted by Satan in the desert, He would not assume an identity He knew to be false. He knew what was written in the books of heaven about His destiny and life. The same cosmic struggle occurs over us each time we are tempted to assume an identity other than the one written about us by the Father in Heaven. Jesus promised a way of escape and He came to destroy the works and schemes of the enemy in my life and yours. Turning our eyes toward Him and focusing on His divine character in us, we will then reflect Him to a lost and dying world.

"This is how love is made complete among us so that we will have confidence on the Day of Judgment: In this world we are like Jesus." (1 John 4:17). As Jesus is, so are we in the world. He is holy and calls us to be holy. He is righteous and calls us to be righteous. He is infused with glory and resurrection power, and so too are we. He is ever doing the Father's will and so too must we!

The Bible tells us that no matter what difficulties or what circumstances we face, we are to bear Christ's likeness. We are to edify and encourage one another just as Jesus did, not tear each other down. God does not want us to only **have** a revelation of Christ, He wants us to **be** a revelation and reflection of Christ. Once we know who Christ is, we will begin to understand who He made us to be.

Our Purpose as Christians

The Bible tells us that our purpose is to be conformed into the image of Christ, so that we can glorify Him in all we do. *"For whom He did foreknow, He also did predestinate to be conformed to the image of His Son"* (Romans 8:29). We are to comfort, encourage, edify and strengthen one another as Jesus would do. Being conformed into Christ's image is the goal of the Christian life. In other words, being born in the spirit at our new birth is just the beginning. We should desire to learn how to walk in the Spirit, how to show forth His Love, and how to live His Life. Our actions should reflect what we already possess in our heart- Jesus! This is the purpose of our existence as Christ's followers. We are to be changed from the inside out, and begin to reflect His likeness and His image. (See Galatians 4:19; Romans 8:29).

We are to love with His Love; share from His wisdom; walk in His power; extend His peace, patience and joy; confront evil with truth, and be His hands and feet to a lost and dying world.

Glorifying God simply means reflecting His likeness in all we do. It means unlearning all our old ways of thinking and doing, and allowing Him to manifest and express His characteristics through us. It means removing every hindrance, every obstacle and every blockage in our life that quenches His Spirit, so that He may be clearly seen through us, just as the Father was perfectly seen through Jesus. As Hebrews 1:3 says, *"Jesus, who was the brightness of His glory and the express image of His person."*

Jesus even went further and said in John 5:31, *"If I bear witness of myself, my witness is not true."* WOW! If Jesus says this of Himself, oh my goodness, how much more must it be true of us! We are to bear witness of God's image, not our own. Jesus lived as a man filled with Holy Spirit and compelled to do the Father's will even unto death. He lived as a man to show us it is possible to be united in fellowship with the Father.

In order to evaluate your own progress towards this end, ask yourself these simple questions: Do I need to surrender my heart to Jesus, repent of my sin, and make Him Lord of my life today? Or, does being a Christian make a difference in my life? Does Christ's character flow forth from me? Do others see the love of Christ and the fruit of the Spirit in me?

Bow down on the inside and ask yourself if you believe these statements and **declare them out loud**: I am a new creation in Christ Jesus. My spirit is created in the image and likeness of God.

I am complete in Christ Jesus. I am righteous in Christ Jesus. I have right standing with God just like I had never done anything wrong. I can do all things through Christ who strengthens me.

I am God's child and a joint-heir with Christ. There is no lack for my God supplies all my needs, in every area of life, according to His riches in glory by Christ Jesus. I have the mind of Christ.

I have an anointing from the Holy One. I will look in the mirror, the Word of God, and see an accurate reflection of myself, and I will never forget who I am or what I look like.

Revisit the diagram in Chapter Six and see what God is showing you now.

#9. Another obstacle that keeps us from enjoying a right relationship with the Father as His son or daughter is not realizing fully that our righteousness is as filthy rags. Any time we think we are the one accomplishing things in our own lives, outside of God's hand and grace, we are fooling ourselves. God holds our very breadth in His hands, counts the hairs on our heard, knows the beginning from the end, and holds all things together by His will. All righteousness belongs to God! He alone is worthy of all praise. We still hold onto mindsets of this world when we applaud our own accomplishments, because without God's mercy in our lives we might find ourselves in the most desperate of situations. Mary Magdaline had the right attitude as she wiped Jesus' feet with her tears. From the one who has been forgiven much, they can love much. If you find yourself forgiven much, you may know full well how far you have fallen, and how far the Lord has raised you up. For others who led a more productive life in this world, it might be harder for you to realize that it was not you who placed you in more comfortable situations, it was God. We all have sinned and fallen short of the glory of God and need forgiveness and a humble and contrite heart before a holy God.

PRAYER TO JEHOVAH TSIDKENU, MY RIGHTEOUSNESS

What lies ahead is far greater than I could ever imagine and I know what You have in store for me is magnificent. I come Lord, I come! Impart to me all that I need to face yet another journey, yet another giant. I know I am precious to You **Jehovah Tsidkenu, My Righteousness**, and that You love me so very much; as I do You. Allow me the privilege Lord to see your reflection clearly, Your glory in the sanctuary. I pray for revelation of Your love so that I would never doubt again. Help me to remember that my righteousness is as filthy rags, but that You have clothed me in your robes of righteousness. I declare and decree that I am ready to face the giants in the land for You are with me. I declare and decree that I will always find You in in the solitude and silence of Your embrace. I declare and decree that I will not allow lusts of the flesh, lust of the eyes, pride of life or selfishness, indignation or offense to rule in my heart. I declare and decree that my body, mind, will and spirit are yielded and consumed by Holy Spirit who empowers me to live a supernatural life. I declare and decree that peace, joy and righteousness are the characteristics of the Kingdom of God and they will rule and reign in my heart all the days of my life. I declare and decree that I will not sow to the flesh and reap ruin and decay, but will sow to the Spirit and from the Spirit reap eternal life.

WALKING IN HIS PURPOSE AND POWER

Chapter X

*If I should find security in all the wrong places, remind me that my circumstances do not define your love. Enable me to speak life and not death over myself and those I love as I shelter my laser focus on Thee. Draw me into Your Holy presence **Kadosh, My Holy One** that your sustenance, grace, mercy, peace, love, and joy are mine. I declare and decree no weapon formed against me will prosper for you are my **Jehovah Metsudhathi, My High Tower**.*

> *"To whom then will you liken me that I would be his equal?" says the Holy One (Kadosh)"* (Isa. 40:25).

> *"The LORD (Jehovah) is my rock, my fortress (Metsudhathi)*
> *and my deliverer; my God is my rock, in whom I take*
> *refuge, my shield and the horn of my salvation, my strong-*
> *hold"* (Ps. 18:2)

The years 2020-2022 were challenging for us all. Many are still reeling from the effects of sickness, loss of loved ones, completely changed routines, devastation of finances, job or home loss, and a myriad of other results. My husband's mother died in October of 2020 at age 98. Someone at a nursing home was pushing her wheelchair, she fell and broke her neck and leg. A few days later she was gone. My own mother died a month later at the age of 90 in another nursing home. They are both sorely missed.

So in the midst of turmoil, strife, unrest, and sorrow, how do we stand? How do we stay strong? How do we as Christ's followers fight the good fight of faith? Each person's journey is different, but the joy set before us can be an anchor for our souls. We must stay fixed in our commitment to seek God with our whole heart, mind and soul in every season. His Kingdom is my reality more fully and strongly than this present age, for this age will pass away but His Word and His Kingdom will never end. We need to learn to walk according to its principles, stand on its promises, and anchor our identity in Jesus alone. I would rather declare and decree all He has said than repeat one word of what man says or what the news says. The Lord told us to occupy until He returns, so doing the next thing was how my past few years went, one day at a time. I prayed for open doors, wrote, served those in need, loved on family and friends as I was able, sewed about eight hundred masks, and sought a deeper walk of faith with Jesus. We are in a new year and things may have gone from bad to worse in the physical realm, but praise God in it all. I always say, He's still on the throne, in control, and nothing surprises Him. I will trust Him through each day, and continue to serve others. I find indescribable peace in serving. It is the divine love song fulfilling my union and fellowship with God.

"Blow on my garden, that its fragrance may spread everywhere. Let my beloved come into his garden and taste its choice fruits" (Song of Solomon 4:16).

"At the place where Jesus was crucified, there was a garden, and in the garden a new tomb, in which no one had ever been laid" (John 19:41).

Our life is in the midst of a garden and we need to die with Christ to live again in it. And once we live again through salvation, there is an assignment for us to fulfill in this garden. What needs to die in the garden of your life so you may live fully for Christ? Until we die to self, and this of course is a life-long commitment of our soul, we will be tempted to boast of things other than Christ crucified. I believe 2020 stripped away a lot of excess from people's lives, causing many to stop and realize that being in control was never in their hands. I pray many looked to God in this season, because He longs for each one to return to His heart. The storms of life come and go. Sometimes we boast in our rich seasons of life, and all the success we have accomplished. Sometimes we boast in our own efforts, surviving the difficult seasons of life. Both are wrong according to the Word, for without the Lord forming us, fashioning us, giving us the breadth of life, and securing our health, we could do nothing apart from Him. He rains blessings on the just and the unjust. He alone is holy. He alone is our strong tower. He alone is to be our boast.

THIS PRESENT STORM

You LORD have quieted our hearts
In the midst of turmoil and fears
You've called us to the deeper things
Beyond the strife and tears

We see your hand above it all
And know Your Presence more
Abiding love is ours each day
As we enter Heaven's door

Embracing your heart for all those you love
To see the sights and sounds of Glory
We'll bow and worship you alone
To fulfill and complete your own story

This plague will pass by your command
For Your Will shall always prevail
So keep your people faithful Lord
As we pass through this mighty gale

BREADTH OF GOD

Voice of Heaven, breadth of God
Shelter us in grace
Keep our hearts and minds in Thee
Less we falter and fail this race

Voice of Heaven, breadth of God
Creation shouts Your Glory
Hold us close with tender care
As we walk out this, our story

Voice of Heaven, breadth of God
Your hand and heart upon our own
Help us walk so near to Thee
That death and life are sown

Voice of Heaven, breadth of God
Jesus' death was our redemption
His resurrection tied to it
Death and life Your conception

You have risen and given life
Our heartbeat but a shadow
Of the drumbeat of heaven's chorus
Your Kingdom's Transition's Glow
Shine Bright!

LESSON 10
Boasting, Holiness, Strong Tower

BOASTING

According to the Book of Daniel in the Old Testament, the Babylonian king Nebuchadnezzar suffered from a mental illness, and lived isolated for seven years, until he acknowledged the power of the one true God. How many years do we wander in our own pride and ignorance until we finally turn to the one true God? Let us explore this question by studying this section of Scripture, and see how God will turn our heart one degree closer to His heart.

Read Daniel chapters 1-4.

Look specifically at chapter four. This story in chapter four is both a tangible event as well as a prophecy, but continues to be a conundrum to many who read it. When Daniel interpreted the dream for Nebuchadnezzar in Daniel 4:24, he told him if he repented from his sin and wickedness then his prosperity might continue. A full year passed, but he did not repent or renounce his sins.

> *Twelve months later, as the king was walking on the roof of the royal palace of Babylon, he said, "Is not this the great Babylon I have built as the royal residence, by my mighty power and for the glory of my majesty? Even as the words were on his lips, a voice came from heaven, "This is what is decreed for you, King Nebuchadnezzar: Your royal authority has been taken from you"* (Dan. 4:29-30).

Perhaps, had Nebuchadnezzar humbled himself, his experience may not have been so severe. Just as the Israelites grumbled and complained in the desert, after being freed from Egypt, an eleven day journey took forty years. I do not know your story, but I am sorry to say mine was similar. Because I focused on what had passed that I could never change, because I grieved over dreams not fulfilled, because I refused to humble myself before God, consequences came into my life that continued to break my will before a holy God. He wants our submission, but more than that He wants our hearts.

Back to Daniel's account. The voice Nebuchadnezzar heard told him that his authority had been removed, and he would be driven away from people and live among wild animals. Sometimes God will break us of our extreme pride and teach us a greater lesson. Nebuchadnezzar was reduced to living like an animal wherein he lost his reason and suffered a lapse of sanity for seven years. There is actually a form of mental illness (oanthropy/insania zoanthropica) in which people think they are animals and imitate them. Scholars believe that Nebuchadnezzar probably suffered from hallucinations, hypochondria, delusions or even neurological disease. Secular history during 582BC and 575BC in Babylon is silent. Personally I suffered years of depression. We allow the enemy of our soul to buffet us unmercifully, because we are too prideful to admit our greater need for God, or our need for forgiveness. When we do not know what the Word of God says, we pretend it is not true. How can we know if we don't read it?

Nebuchadnezzar's kingdom and sanity were returned to him after the seven year period, and he glorified God as he had previously been told to do. He was very mindful that what God does is right and just (see Daniel 4:37).

God is the author of everything and able to humble those who walk in pride. We have no power that God did not allow us to have. We have no wealth that God did not allow us to achieve. We have no talents that God did not allow us to display. We have no family that God did not allow us to love. We have no home that God did not allow us to live in. We have no education that God did not allow us to retain. We have no provision God did not allow us to partake of. He is author of all.

The prophetic view is that God allows leaders to exercise their influence for both good and evil, but when the appointed time is completed their authority will be removed. Then all nations of the earth will bow down in reverence to the Lord of Lords and the King of Kings.

> *Repent, then, and turn to God, so that your sins may be wiped out, that times of refreshing may come from the Lord, and that he may send the Messiah, who has been appointed for you—even Jesus. Heaven must receive him until the time comes for God to restore everything, as he promised long ago through his holy prophets"* (Acts 3:19-21).

Read and write out the following Scriptures and then answer the following questions:

Jer. 31:34

2 Cor. 11:30

2 Cor. 12:9

Phil. 2:16

- After reading these Scriptures, how did the Holy Spirit speak to your heart?

- What boasting might you need to eliminate from your speech?

"The tongue has the power of life and death, and those who love it will eat its fruit" (Prov. 18:21).

- What other negative words should you stop speaking over yourself, your family, your church and your community?

- What does 'eat its fruit' mean in this passage?

HOLINESS

> *"To whom then will you liken me that I would be his equal?" says the Holy One (Kadosh)"* (Isa. 40:25).

In John 17 Jesus is praying that the Father will make his followers united and holy. It's the longest recorded prayer of Jesus. Take a moment to read John 17.

Our Creator knows exactly what we need to live for him and fulfill his purpose.

- Take some time to really ask God what His thoughts of you are and His purpose.

Many people fear death, but if Jesus destroyed death, then He also destroyed our fear of death. If I am truly alive in Christ and in his Kingdom now, then death is a transition from one state to another.

He has promised to prepare a room for me and so much more. As we disengage ourselves from the things of this world, and place our heart, mind and will in heaven now, our transition there will be so peaceful. It is the fire and wrath of a holy God against an unregenerated soul that should be feared. It is this side of heaven we get to choose to love God or not. I pray many will come to realize that waiting to see what is after this life is not a very good strategy of life.

The thought of Jesus actually praying for us to be holy blows my mind. The Greek word for holy is 'Hagianzein' and means to be holy, set apart, sanctified, consecrated, devoted, and made different. We are all in a process of being made holy as we diligently seek God. The problem is many times we think "I know God, I have given my life to Christ and to His counsel and will in my life". Even Satan knows who Jesus is. It is not all about just **knowing Him**, it's about **following Him**. To follow requires movement, directionality, and forward momentum in the Kingdom. Yes, we are saved by grace, but our response to God's love is as an active participant in that relationship. It is not a passive and complacent waiting until we get to heaven stance. There is work in the garden of God's Kingdom to be done. Here I am Lord, send me.

- Is that your cry every day or do you have mixture in your life with the things of this world consuming your thoughts, activities, energy and will?

- In what areas do you find 'mixture' with this world? Identify how they are unhealthy or are distracting you from following things God has laid on your heart in the past.

God has set us apart '**from**' the world. He wants us to be different. What a calming balm to know that different is OK. This world's definitions of us pale in comparison to who God says we are. My Creator has sole right to define me. One way God sets us apart is by His Word of truth, and all the things He has said about us. Remember these statements from earlier in our reading:

I am a new creation in Christ Jesus. My spirit is created in the image and likeness of God.

I am complete in Christ Jesus.

I am righteous in Christ Jesus. I have right standing with God just like I'd never done anything wrong.

I can do all things through Christ who strengthens me.

I am God's child and a joint-heir with Christ.

There is no lack for my God supplies all my needs, in every area of life, according to his riches in glory by Christ Jesus.

I have the mind of Christ.

I have an anointing from the Holy One.

I will look in the mirror, the Word of God, and see an accurate reflection of myself, and I will never forget who I am or what I look like.

Because God is Holy, He longs for me to know who I am in Him and also to be holy.

He has also set us apart **'for'** the World, that others might see the light of Christ in us. We are glory carriers and His treasured possessions. (Deut. 7). He has set us apart by His grace for His glory.

- Read the following Scriptures and record what the Lord is speaking to you:

Matthew 6:9 -

John 17:16-17 -

Col. 3:1-5 -

John 17:18 -

Rom. 1:1 -

John 17:19 -

Eph. 2 –

The same God who justifies us, also sanctifies us. The same God who made us holy at salvation, makes us holy as we seek Him daily.

STRONG TOWER

> *"The LORD (Jehovah) is my rock, my fortress (Metsudhathi) and my deliverer; my God is my rock, in whom I take refuge, my shield and the horn of my salvation, my strong-hold"* (Ps. 18:2).

- Define the following terms:

Deliverer-

Refuge-

Shield-

Stronghold / Strong Tower -

- Can you recall a time or season when God delivered you out of a difficult circumstance or trial?

- Maybe you came through something, but never really acknowledged God's hand at work in your circumstance. Can you reflect on it now, and thank Him for bringing you through? If not, why not?

- Do you think it might be a trust issue? Perhaps, you are still placing the results in your own efforts or in the efforts of others.

Map out some highs and lows in your life both circumstantially and spiritually on a type of roller-coaster line. Think and pray about your journey of faith and see if you can identify times when God was your Deliverer, Refuge, Shield and/or Strong Tower.

> *"For you have been my refuge, a strong tower against the foe"* (Ps. 61:3).

- What foe are you battling in your life?

God wants to be your refuge and strength. Release the battle to the Lord and let Him fight for yo

#10. Another obstacle that keeps us from enjoying a right relationship with the Father as His son or daughter is not realizing fully that our boast is to be in Christ alone; we cannot take credit for one

breadth of our life. He alone is holy and He alone is our strong tower. He formed us in our mother's womb. He breathed the breadth of life into our lungs. He ordained who our parents would be. He set us on a course, with books written in heaven about us, that we would choose life, that we would choose Christ, that we would choose God above our own will to fulfill the destiny He had planned for us. Salvation is a free gift, and as we partner with the Holy Spirit, we can experience joys unspeakable. Allowing Holy Spirit to move in and through us is for God's glory. When we take credit for any of the gifts of life God has given us, then we deny Him the glory due Him. Whether it is a career, our intelligence, our finances, our family,–whatever good gifts they may be- NOTHING comes to us that is not given by God. Any evil in our life is from the pit of hell and the enemy, and sometimes from our own wrong choices. May our only boast be in Jesus Christ. Father, Son and Spirit are Holy and He calls us to be holy. We take on the characteristics of our Father God, because He is our parent. He alone is Holy, and He calls us to be holy as He is holy. And when the enemy assails, we run to Christ because He is our strong tower; our tower of refuge and strength. He is our tower allowing us to see from a higher perspective and discern the enemy's tactics.

PRAYER TO JEHOVAH KADOSH, MY HOLY ONE, TO JEHOVAH METSUDHATHI, MY HIGH TOWER

My circumstances do not define Your love, they shelter my laser focus on Thee, and draw me into Your Holy presence **Kadosh, My Holy One**, Your sustenance, grace, mercy, peace, love, and joy. I come! I declare and decree no weapon formed against me will prosper for You are my **Jehovah Metsudhathi., My High Tower.** I look only to You Jehovah Kadosh to decree Your holiness alone within me; my righteousness is as filthy rags. As You are faithful, You are forming me in the image of Your son Jesus. I pray for more of Holy Spirit to fulfill the call of God in my life and be a light in this dark world. Jehovah Metsudhathi, You are my strong tower when the storms of life rage and the waves billow over me. I cling to you. I declare and decree that Your strength is my strength as I trust in Your unfailing love and presence in my life. I declare and decree that You allow me to see from the heights, discern the schemes of the enemy, and draw near to Your presence. I wait and watch for what You will say, and record revelations revealed.

Chapter XI

Painting by Barbara Dalton

Forgive me Lord should I boast in any name but Yours. I declare and decree, **Jehovah Nissi, The Lord My Banner,** *that my mind and boast will be the mind and boast of Christ alone. I declare and decree that my mouth will be an instrument of Your peace, and my helmet of salvation will guard me from every lie of the enemy. To* **Jehovah Magen, The Lord My Shield,** *I declare and decree that Holy Spirit within me will be all consuming and the belt of Truth will bind my armor. I declare and decree the righteousness of Christ is my breastplate and guards me against the arrows of the enemy. I declare and decree Jesus has shod my feet with the gospel of peace and many will come to salvation because of my obedience to the call.*

> *"Moses built an altar and named it The LORD is My Banner (Johovah Nissi)"* (Ex. 17:15).

"Blessed are you, Israel! Who is like you, a people saved by the LORD? He is your shield and helper and your glorious sword. Your enemies will cower before you, and you will tread on their heights" (Deut. 33:29).

Consider His Glory

Between the seasons and these times
God stops us all and says, "Just pause."
Consider My Glory, Consider My Love
Fight for My just cause

But we wander as we wonder
This pinnacle of abundant grace
Consider My Glory, Consider My Love
Struggling in life's arduous race

Silence of the calm; raging of the storm
Riding both trough and crest of waves
Consider My Glory, Consider My Love
Touching the ONE who truly saves

Years end and years begin
His faithfulness forever sure
Consider My Glory, Consider My Love
Seeing beyond My open door

Between the seasons and these times
God stops us all and says, "Just come."
Consider My Glory, Consider My Love
Hearing only Heaven's drum

When is the last time you witnessed a miracle or experienced awe in God's Presence? I Praise God that those occurrences in my life are increasing. The eternal atmospheres have shifted as we approach the last days. God is pouring out His Spirit on our sons and daughters. Miracles, signs and wonders are following those who believe in increasing measure. May we walk in His presence all the days of our lives. Our Abba Father loves us so much, and leans over the banister of heaven to hear our hearts. I have seen miracles in Romania, on the streets of our city, in our churches and in the prison. Recently, in the fall of 2021, I was with a team praying over a man with a torn rotator cuff, and within minutes he was healed. That was a Sunday; by his scheduled surgery that Tuesday, he was continuing to walk in his healing. When the doctor did some tests and saw him Tuesday, he said the man was completely healed. The surgery was cancelled.

Recently a woman came to our healing rooms for prayer with chronic back pain that had burdened her for a long time. After prayer, she was released from all pain and now six months later she is still pain free. Around the same time, I was street witnessing and prayed with a tough looking young man. He was trying to fight addictions and old lifestyles. As we prayed, God softened his heart and he wept. Only Holy Spirit can move in the hearts and minds and bodies of people in those ways. May we consider more the glory of God housed within these broken vessels of ours, and live courageous bold lives.

LESSON 11 KNOWING OUR DESTINY

"And he who searches our hearts knows the mind of the Spirit, because the Spirit intercedes for God's people in accordance with the will of God. And we know that in all things God works for the good of those who love him, who have been called according to his purpose. For those God foreknew he also predestined to be conformed to the image of his Son, that he might be the firstborn among many brothers and sisters. And those he predestined, he also called; those he called, he also justified; those he justified, he also

glorified. What, then, shall we say in response to these things? If God is for us, who can be against us? He who did not spare his own Son, but gave him up for us all—how will he not also, along with him, graciously give us all things? Who will bring any charge against those whom God has chosen? It is God who justifies. Who then is the one who condemns? No one. Christ Jesus who died—more than that, who was raised to life—is at the right hand of God and is also interceding for us. Who shall separate us from the love of Christ? Shall trouble or hardship or persecution or famine or nakedness or danger or sword? As it is written: "For your sake we face death all day long; we are considered as sheep to be slaughtered." No, in all these things we are more than conquerors through him who loved us. For I am convinced that neither death nor life, neither angels nor demons, neither the present nor the future, nor any powers, neither height nor depth, nor anything else in all creation, will be able to separate us from the love of God that is in Christ Jesus our Lord" (Rom. 8:27-39).

I am so blessed knowing that Jesus is interceding on my behalf according to the will of God. His banner over me is love. He shields me in the faith He imparts to me. Being called according to His purpose is both a privilege and a responsibility. Meditate on and study the above Scripture until it saturates your soul. Our ultimate mandate, as we seek God first, is to look more and more like Jesus until we are one with Him in glory. There is a biblical process of looking more and more like Jesus that is delineated in the above Scriptures. We will begin by understanding the following definitions.

Foreknew- In Romans 8:29 "**foreknew**" is the Greek word proegnō, which translates as "to know beforehand". In Amos 3:2 "known" is the Hebrew word ya·da'·ti, which translates as "chosen".[15]

Remember that to foreknow can be defined in two ways, one is philosophical and the other biblical. Philosophically, foreknowledge is simply to know something beforehand. If we bring this definition to Romans 8:29-30 it simply means God knows the end from the beginning and saw all those that would choose to follow Him. He foreknew that they would choose Him. Though true, the biblical definition shows that God, based solely on His sovereign grace, chooses or elects to set His affection on men, regenerate them and open their hearts to His truth. I believe at some point in every life God extends His hand toward them. He grants them a measure of faith to truly know and receive His love. He has planted eternity in every heart revealing it through creation, His Word, and the gospel being shared. It is up to each one, whether or not they choose, to accept His love. We can love someone dearly, but if they refuse to accept our love and walk away from relationship with us, then that is an expression of their free will. The same is true with God's love. People have to understand that if we say someone is 'lost' or 'broken' there's really no accountability on their part. The greater truth is that they have willfully, intentionally, and deliberately made a decision to walk away from Father God's love. Once they can admit that to themselves, transformation of the soul can occur. Taking accountability for our own decisions can bring true repentance and healing.

"You (Israel) only have I known among all the families of the earth" (Amos 3:2). Does God not know all the people of the earth? Of course He does. Hebrews 4:13 tells us that *"nothing is hidden from Him."* So what does this verse in Amos actually mean? God chose to set His favor and affection on Israel, out of all the families of the earth, but that does not negate his love for all mankind.

Research the meaning of *know* in Gen. 4:1.

Before the world was made, God set His affection upon His people. God intimately chooses and knows His people, just as a husband knows his wife. In Revelations we read about the Church as the Bride of Christ. Research how a Jewish wedding is similar to and a foreshadowing of Jesus' second coming. Share what you learn with your group if you are participating in one, or share with a friend.

Predestined- in Christianity, the doctrine that God has eternally chosen those whom he intends to save. It means to determine beforehand, ordain, to limit in advance or to decree from eternity.[16]

Theological scholars have written books on this topic and not the scope of this work. Suffice it to say God is omnipotent and knows the end from the beginning. Though we have free will, he knows the choices men will make.

Conformed- In Greek 'suschēmatizō' translates to conform one's self; one's mind and character to another's pattern or to fashion one's self after another.[17]

Scripture calls us to be transformed in our minds to the will and obedience of Christ. We pattern our lives after the one who came to save us, Jesus Christ. His banner over us is love, and his shield is one of protection and faith.

Called–This word, 'qari' means to call out or invite, address by name or those that are bidden.[18]

Each believed is called to hear the voice of their shepherd and master. He calls us by name and we either accept his invitation or reject it. Once we do, we either follow the rule of Satan and his kingdom, or the rule of Jesus as He calls us ever deeper into His Kingdom life-style, thinking, peace, joy and righteousness. We continue to listen for Jesus' voice, all the days of our lives, and He directs our steps for his ultimate glory.

Justified–This word come from the Greek word dikaioo (pronounced dik-ah-yo'-o). It means to render righteous or for one to be as he/she ought to be. It can also mean to show one to be righteous. Lastly it carries the thought to declare or pronounce one to be just and righteous as they ought to be.[19]

To summarize, the concept of Biblical justification is an act and expression of God's grace. It is when a guilty sinner like you or me puts their faith in Christ, and is judicially acquitted in the courtroom of heaven by God. We are made right with God by the atoning blood of Jesus Christ, and his sacrifice for us on the cross. He bore the sin, guilt, shame and penalty we deserved. Because of what Jesus did, you are made whole and right before a holy God.

Glorified – From the Greek word doxazō glorified carries the idea to think, suppose, or be of the opinion. It means to praise, extol, magnify, celebrate or to honor, do honor to, or hold in honor. It also means to make glorious, adorn with luster, and clothe with splendor. In the richness of this definition it also means to impart glory to something, render it excellent; to make renowned, render illustrious; to cause the dignity and worth of some person or thing to become manifest and acknowledged.[20]

What do you notice about this definition?

"And there came unto me one of the seven angels which had the seven vials full of the seven last plagues, and talked with me, saying, Come hither, I will show thee the bride, the Lamb's wife. And he carried me away in the spirit to a great and high mountain, and showed me that great city, the holy Jerusalem, descending out of heaven from God, having the glory of God: and her light [was] like unto a stone most precious, even like a jasper stone, clear as crystal" (Rev. 21:9-11).

• Who experienced this revelation?

- What is this portion of Scripture describing?

- Have you ever experienced the glory of God?

- Do you think God still manifests himself to his people? (Remember, He changes not!)

God had a plan before one word from his lips created the universe. We see in Genesis that the foundations of His Kingdom are laid one day at a time. Oh, that we could live our days with such a steady focus and tread; letting today's manna feed us for the day. Our Sovereign God opens Scripture portraying His *realm*, His *reign*, and His *regency*. He ends Scripture in Revelation with the same portrayal. He existed before time began and the scope of His rule or *realm* transcends and exceeds this physical realm we encounter. He calls us ever higher. He existed before all creation and His expanse far outshines it. He encompasses it all by virtue of His role as Creator.

His *reign*, the power by which He rules, was creatively designed by His own hand and the counsel of the Trinity. He designed man's reign over the earth as well. Sin brought havoc into creation as it was originally intended to exist. This divine reign of God however is still exercised by Jesus' spoken Word, His divine will, and His magnificent works. God's nature never changed though man's had. We have to understand that God's very nature, spirit and dunamis power reside within us as we exercise our reign in His Kingdom on earth as it is in heaven. We do this as we walk in Holy Spirit's counsel. God creatively designs our lives prior to our birth and our perfect eternal destiny is written in the books of heaven about us. It is up to us to choose His destiny over what we perceive it to be outside His kingdom. By accepting Christ His ultimate purpose will be done on the earth as it is in heaven. The fact that He foreknows it, is only because of His omnipotence as an all-knowing God. This does not negate our free will, but when we willingly choose to follow Him, the divine plan is brought into alignment and perfected in us.

God's *regency* resides in His holiness. This is His authority to rule as He existed at creation and created all things to be good, revealing His holy nature. If God's regency resides in his holiness, then we can only take our rightful place in His Kingdom by being holy as He is holy. He gave this created thought to mankind to be used for good, and even Jesus said we would do greater works than he. He gave mankind authority over all his creation; in salvation that authority is then given back to man. God is creation's King and all authority flows from the Father, Son and Spirit. Jesus is the Alpha and Omega and all creation will return to His hand to be judged. May we as His bride make ourselves ready! May we carry the mantel of His love as we speak the Word of God in boldness and power, fulfilling God's divine will in our lives, and performing magnificent works for His glory.

So how is this possible? Well the Word has a lot to say about this. In Isaiah 61:3 we read "...*and provide for those who grieve in Zion—to bestow on them a crown of beauty instead of ashes, the oil of joy instead of mourning, and a **garment of praise** instead of a **spirit of despair**. They will be called oaks of righteousness, a planting of the LORD for the display of his splendor.*" This is a pivotal Scripture in understanding that when this word said "*spirit of despair*", it is talking about a demonic spirit of despair, heaviness, and weight. I truly believe the church of Jesus Christ needs to rise up and attack this spirit of the enemy with the Word of God in our mouths. This demonic spirit is oppressing not only our churches, but individuals as well. The enemy of our souls has strategic weapons to destroy God's people, and he is using 'despair' to do it. The word 'heaviness' in Greek means to be weighed down, great sorrow or sadness, to be bitter or dejected. More teenagers were admitted to our emergency rooms over the past few years with suicidal thoughts than at any other time in history. Our church doors were closed and people were scattered, just as the Jewish nation was scattered in ancient times. This despairing spirit is also a devouring spirit trying to take things away from God's people. Families have been split apart and destinies all but destroyed. We have to understand that despair is more than an emotion; it begins as a thought, becomes a focus, is conceived in sin and then it leads to death. That is the progression of all destroying sin. We have a thought planted by Satan, it becomes our desire or focus, is then fully conceived as a corruptible seed and leads us towards death and destruction.

Now look at the phrase *"garment of praise"* in Isa. 61:3. This whole portion of Scripture hinges on these two phrases because we will not know the oil of joy or gladness deep in our spirits until we get this right. Notice praise is a garment to cover oneself or envelop oneself in. Praise is not so much a song, but rather an attitude of thanksgiving and worship in our minds. It is a state of constant awareness that our God dwells in the praises of his people, and thanksgiving is the key that ushers us to praise. Look at Psalm 100:3-4 *"Know that the LORD is God. It is he who made us, and we are his; we are his people, the sheep of his pasture.* **Enter his gates with thanksgiving and his courts with praise; give thanks to him and praise his name.**"

In 2 Timothy 3: 1-4 we see a severe thought- *But mark this: There will be terrible times in the last days. People will be lovers of themselves, lovers of money, boastful, proud, abusive, disobedient to their parents,* **ungrateful,** *unholy, without love, unforgiving, slanderous, without self-control, brutal, not lovers of the good, treacherous, rash, conceited, lovers of pleasure rather than lovers of God."* For as severe as each of those eighteen behaviors are, may Jesus' bride, His church, not be participating in any of these. It is especially imperative that we not be ungrateful or unthankful. Praise unlocks the presence of God and opens fellowship with the Father in his throne room. If thanksgiving unlocks praise, let us be a thankful people. The enemy wants nothing more than to shut up the voice of the one who has truth in them. We thank God for what He has already done while we praise Him for what He is yet to do. Thanksgiving unlocks the gate to praise, and praise unlocks the gate to God's Presence. His presence then floods us with joy. God lives in the midst of praising attitudes and keeps us from the spirit of heaviness. Praise declares what God has yet to do, as we prophesy and declare our future, both here and in heaven. It builds our faith, translating us into our future and oneness with our Abba Father. The earth is the Lord's.

God is above and greater than any situation in which you may find yourself. Begin to thank him for all you do have. "*I will extol the LORD at all times; **his praise will always be on my lips.** I will glory in the LORD; let the afflicted hear and rejoice. Glorify the LORD with me; let us exalt his name together*" (Ps. 34:1b-3). Challenge yourself to keep praise always on your lips as David did here. See if you are not transformed in your spiritual growth. Remember too, God chose David to be king. Perhaps, because David knew how to praise God. David had a grateful heart. We are called kings and priests unto God, with Jesus as our high priest. Oh, that we would praise Him!

Thanksgiving is the language of heaven and praise is its symphony. They usher in the Father's love and joy in abundance. We cannot speak both complaints and praise from the same mouth. Fresh water and stagnant water do not flow from the same source. Our words matter! They matter to God, they matter to the spiritual atmosphere, and they matter to your own life and the lives you influence. We influence others either positively or negatively and our words hold the power of life and death. Read and study the following Scriptures and may the Spirit of the living God speak to your heart.

Either write out these Scriptures or comment on what you learn:

Deut. 30:19

Prov. 18:21

Ps. 56:13

Prov. 10:16

Jer. 21:8

John 5:24

Rom. 4:25

Rom. 5:17

Rom. 6:13

Rom. 8:2

2 Cor. 2:16

Phil. 1:20

Read 1 Cor. 15:35-58.

What is to be the glory of man? (See vs. 41-49)

Notice verse 53. What are we to clothe ourselves in?

Are we to die daily to self as we are formed in Christ's image?

What is God showing you after reading these Scriptures?

What questions do you still have? Share with an accountability partner or group.

God has so much more for us if we would just keep our eyes off the world and on His Kingdom. Praise keeps us from looking back. The Lord wants all of ourselves, not a portion, not a segmented life. No one who puts their hand to the plow of his work should look back. (Read 1 Kings 19). Prayer matters, our words matter, God's Word matters in our mouths.

If you know any history of the Dunkirk evacuation of 1940, you will know that when King George VI called his nation to prayer, miracles happened as a result. Over 300,000 Allied soldiers who had been trapped by the Nazis were rescued. It was called a miracle, but it was really a series of miracles. As people prayed, Nazis troop suddenly stopped their offense in their tracks, a heavy protective cloud cover lasted for days, the English Channel grew extraordinarily calm, and hundreds of tiny boats coming from all directions helped rescue troops.

Prayer and praise blind the enemy. That is the oil on our shield of faith. Holy Spirit's oil of prayer and praise lubricate our shield to protect us from the enemy's attacks. When we lose vision, we will not see the glory of God. We must not let circumstances get in our spirit or define our destiny. Praise will stop a plague and loose the glory of God as He turns around the impossible. Out of the abundance of what is stored up in our hearts our mouths will speak. What are we storing up in our minds and hearts? Is it the Lord's presence, His Spirit, and His Word or is it the negative thinking of this world's systems? Loose life from your lips, not death. Praise your way to victory. If you find yourself in a tough place, thank and praise God, then wait to see what He will do.

Our destiny is to use our mouth in prayer and praise to affect lives and impact nations. It is still occurring today, but you will not see it on the national news. Live in the supernatural and you will see supernatural things. *"If anyone speaks, they should do so as one who speaks the very words of God. If anyone serves, they should do so with the strength God provides, so that in all things God may be praised through Jesus Christ. To him be the glory and the power for ever and ever. Amen"* (1 Peter 4:11). Ask God for the grace to both praise and obey Him. Remember what Romans 8:18-19 tells us, *"I consider that our present sufferings are not worth comparing with the glory that will be revealed in us. For the creation waits in eager expectation for the children of God to be revealed."*

#11. Another obstacle that keeps us from enjoying a right relationship with the Father as His son or daughter is not understanding our destiny and the power of our words.

> *And we know that all things work together for good to those who love God, to those who are the called according to [His] purpose. For whom He foreknew, He also predestined [to be] conformed to the image of His Son, that He might be the firstborn among many brethren. Moreover whom He predestined, these He also called; whom He called, these He also justified; and whom He justified, these He also glorified"* (Rom. 8:28-30).

In that continuum of spiritual growth, where do you find yourself? In which concept has the enemy held you bound in doubt, confusion or silence? It is time to clarify your destiny based on the truth of God's Word; written, read and spoken in His divine plan for you. If we have accepted Jesus as Lord and Savior, we will all be conforming to Christ's image while on this earth if we truly pursue Christ's righteousness and holiness. Then Christ's bride, His Ecclesia, His spotless church, will be holy and ready at His return. But consider His calling on your life, know your justification through the Blood of Jesus, and walk in the 'express image of His love' on this earth. His banner over us is love. His shield is our faith declared and decreed against the forces of evil. If we truly understand Who Jesus is, what He came to give us, and that He and the Father love us so much, our lives will reflect His character and nature. Our words hold life even as Jesus is the Word within us. It is His work in and through us, but we must partner with Him in discipline, prayer, worship and obedience. The faith of Christ imparted to us by a Holy God is the faith rising up in His Bride. Let us not just look to others to be ready for Christ's return, let us, ourselves, truly be ready! True holiness within will have great influence in the world as we boldly and courageously speak it out. Jesus asked if He would find faith on the earth at His return. Let it begin with you and me.

PRAYER TO JEHOVAH NISSI, THE LORD MY BANNER AND TO JEHOVAH MAGEN, THE LORD MY SHIELD

I declare and decree, **Jehovah Nissi, The Lord My Banner**, that my mind will be the mind of Christ, my mouth will be an instrument of Your peace, and my helmet of salvation will guard me from every lie of the enemy. To **Jehovah Magen, The Lord My Shield**, I declare and decree that Holy Spirit within me will be all consuming and the belt of Truth will bind my armor. I declare and decree the righteousness of Christ is my breastplate and guards me against the arrows of the enemy. I declare and decree Jesus has shod my feet with the gospel of peace and many will come to salvation because of my obedience to the call. I declare and decree Your Holy Spirit within me will be all consuming, and the belt of truth will bind my armor. I declare and decree the righteousness of Christ is my breastplate, and guards me against the arrows of the enemy. Your banner over me is love. You knew me before I was conceived in my mother's womb, while the books written of my life were penned by Your hand. You predestined to love me with eternal love, and lavish on me the hopes of a loving parent. You gave me free will and I confess that my decisions have altered Your plan for me over the years. Now that I have turned my face towards You, You are conforming me to the image of Your Son Jesus. That knowledge alone is almost more than I can conceive. I Praise You Lord and am overjoyed in your love. May my thanksgiving be the key to open doors of praise in my life, and then may that praise usher me into the courts of heaven. May your glory be seen in all the earth through Your bride, the church, of which I am a part. Grant us Lord a new baptism of courage. Let our witness of your love, grace, mercy and peace go forth into this broken and dying world. Use the declarations and decrees of our mouth to shift atmospheres, and demolish the armies of hell as You shield us. You promised us if we would open our mouth, You would fill it. May the words of our mouths and meditations of our hearts bring You praise and honor. May the declarations we make be of Your Word, and then we will see atmospheres shift over our lives and those we minister to. Our words hold the power of life, may we never yield to using our mouths to declare death. Grant us more of Your Holy Spirit.

Chapter XII

Painting by Robert Stover

*'**Or Goyim, A Light to the Nations** I hold strong and steady the shield of faith and proclaim the great works that God has done. When I feel unqualified, I pick up my sword, the Word of God, and take the land before me in the Blood of the Lamb and in His name, that name that surpasses every other name, Jesus the Christ, my Living Lord. Amen*

"I am the LORD, I have called you in righteousness, I will also hold you by the hand and watch over you, and I will appoint you as a covenant to the people, as a light to the nations ('Or Goyim)" (Isa. 43:6).

Your Worth Within Me

The worth that is within me is from the Lord's own hand
In Christ Jesus only will I forever stand!
He brought me out of darkness into a marvelous light
He clothed me in His righteousness to get ready for the fight
He filled my path with strength and grace
Gave me a servant soldier's heart to run life's race
Used me even when my own dreams were gone
Replaced them all with His new song
He's taken me from miry places
Given me prayers for unseen faces
For years He's gathered all my tears
And turned them into joy
How could I help but sing His praises?
How could I help but love His name?
The worth that is within me is from the Lord's own hand
In Christ Jesus only will I forever stand!

Jehovah Magen, The Lord My Shield, sustains me as I go forth into His Kingdom work and will, both now and into eternity. As Jesus is my Alpha and Omega, I believe He is both my beginning and end. He is both the Creator of my soul and receives me to Himself when I pass from this earth. So I thought it appropriate to circle back, in a way, to how this book began. God holds me in love from the beginning of my life until its transition from this realm. The Lord reveals mysteries to me as I continue to seek Him, to know Him intimately, and to worship Him without restraint.

"This, then, is how you ought to regard us: as servants of Christ and as those entrusted with the mysteries God has revealed" (I Cor. 4:1).

The secret things belong to the LORD our God, but the things revealed belong to us and to our children forever, that we may follow all the words of this law. I come from His hand and I will return to it" (Deut. 29:29).

The following page is one download I received from the Lord in 2020 as I was studying Genesis 2:10-14. It is how the Lord allows me to see greater truths by digging deeper. I read that one Scripture, and it led me down a path of word study that was so impactful to me. The meanings of the four rivers mentions there and all the lands the rivers flow through depict our world and its systems. They depict how the living waters of God's truth, Spirit, and Word impact a fallen world. I have found myself within each of these lands at different times in my life, as the waters of Christ's river of life have led me, refreshed me, and guided me in ways that I will be forever grateful. When I saw these hidden truths within the meanings of the Hebrew words, I knew God was calling me to share it. I shared it with two of my home groups and God used it for His glory. The Lord Jehovah Magen, as my Shield, allows me to travel in realms I would not by nature travel in, but because of His empowering Holy Spirit and His continual protection I now can. He enables me to do all things as Christ strengthens me. I can minister, and you can too, to the fallen human condition of man in the land of pain and sorrow, in the land of darkness and lies, in the land of mixture of good and evil, and in the land of religious systems. Let's take this final journey together through these lands and discover how our God will water our souls and the souls of others because He is so able to shield us on our way, as we follow His way! He ever goes before us.

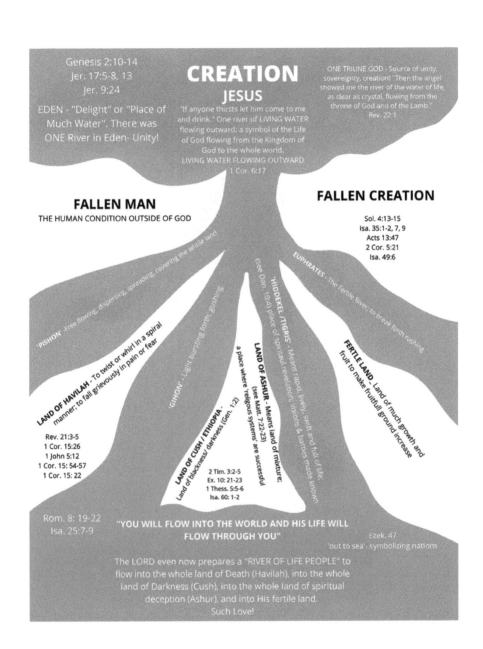

LESSON 12

The Holy Spirit takes the things of Christ and shows them to us. These words of Paul are so very precious, "*He that is **joined** unto the Lord is **one Spirit**"* (I Cor. 6:17). We are joined, as one person, to the Lord as we give ourselves to Him. In our unity with Christ, we are actually one Spirit with Him. It is His life living through us, not us just living for Him; see the difference? As we are coheirs with Christ, our union brings us to a place of one Spirit and one river of living water rushing forth from the high holy realm of the Kingdom of God.

EDEN

"A river watering the garden flowed from Eden; from there it was separated into four headwaters. The name of the first is the Pishon; it winds through the entire land of Havilah, where there is gold. (The gold of that land is good; aromatic resin and onyx are also there.) The name of the second river is the Gihon; it winds through the entire land of Cush. The name of the third river is the Tigris; it runs along the east side of Ashur. And the fourth river is the Euphrates" (Gen. 2:10-14).

This Scripture gripped my heart one day in the middle of my devotions, and I could not leave it until I knew the meanings of each of these rivers and lands. Word meanings is one way I like to study the Word. As I investigated further, I was amazed at what the Lord revealed to me through this living Word. I spent hours dissecting this portion of Genesis. My prayer is that you will discover the joy of dissecting the Word for deeper truths as well. Keep asking: What? Who? Why? When? How? – The journey is so fun!

In the opening chapters of the Bible we are told about the river God put in the Garden of Eden. This original river depicted the oneness of God and man in divine relationship. As it flowed out of the garden into the whole sin-fallen earth, it divided and went in four directions. This is a type, or symbol, of the life and Spirit of God, flowing out from the Kingdom of God to the whole earth. The nature of God's wonderful river of life is that it flows *outward*. Ezekiel once had a vision of a river that flowed out of the temple, and got deeper and deeper as it flowed out to the sea, symbolizing the nations; and it healed the sea or the nations (Ez. 47). Thank God that this river now flows! The life of Jesus Christ is flowing as a river out from the throne room of God. *"On the last and greatest day of the festival, Jesus stood and said in a loud voice, "Let anyone who is thirsty come to me and drink"* (John 7:37).

In Eden, which means "delight" or "place of much water"[21], is where the beautiful garden was that God created for Adam and Eve. I love that it means place of much water, for this is where the Lord walked with His creation. The original river in Eden signifies unity of God and man; a truly blissful relationship. God is the source of all life and this place was one of unity, sovereignty, creation in all its glory, and above all God's presence with man. The Trinity, in their fullness, was intimately involved in loving Adam and Eve. Is not this the utopia we all long for in the depths of our spirits, to truly be one with God? This one river flowed outward and was a symbol of life, watering and nourishing all that lived. Even as mankind fell from relationship with God, it was love and life that still flowed from the Father's throne to His creation, in spite of their failures.

Jesus, as our living water, flowed out of this heavenly realm into the earthly realm to bring life to a fallen world after Adam and Eve sinned. The handprint of Christ's coming for the first time was etched throughout the Old Testament. He stands at the demarcation line between a Holy God and a sinful people. His Spirit, present and active in the Old Testament through the covenant of law, guided man to see truth as a guide, back to the Father's heart. Jesus, Immanuel with us, the Word became flesh dwelt among us in the New Testament of the new covenant of grace. His Spirit empowering His people to go forth in power to defeat the enemy of their souls, just as Jesus did. Jesus came to defeat the works of the enemy, and so too can we. He empowers us for His glory within each of the lands we will study here.

> *"Then the angel showed me a river with the water of life, clear as crystal, flowing from the throne of God and of the Lamb"* (Rev. 22:1).

> *Jesus replied, "If you only knew the gift God has for you and who you are speaking to, you would ask me, and I would give you living water"* (John 4:10).

> *"For my people have done two evil things; they have abandoned me, the fountain of living water. And they have dug for themselves cracked cisterns that can hold no water at all"* (Jer. 2:13)!

Envision for a moment the Garden of Eden. If you draw or paint try to depict it. If not, try to use words to describe what you think it might have been like.

- Reread the Scriptures above. Research something unique about the nature of water and share with your group. What spiritual significance might that have?

- How can we better experience "the gift God has for us" (John 4:10)?

The following rivers and lands exemplify the state of fallen man, the human condition outside of God's presence. The living waters of Christ's Spirit flowing in them represents salvation, sanctification and consecration depicting how we are called. Called as God's chosen people, to spread the life refreshing aroma of Christ. Isaiah 43:6 reads *""I, the LORD, have called you in righteousness; I will take hold of your hand. I will keep you and will make you to be a covenant for the people and a light for the Gentiles,"* Holy Spirit within us is truly divine life giving water and light; the truth, peace, joy and righteousness found in the gospel. These living words and truths traverse the lands of sorrow, darkness, Babylon, and His church.

Let us take a look at each river and each land it runs through.

THE RIVER OF PISHON IN THE LAND OF HAVILAH

Pishon means freely flowing, dispersing, spreading, encompassing the whole land, revolve, or surround. It is the idea in Hebrew of providential turn of affairs, or extension of the mouth. The Land that Pishon flowed into was Havilah. Havilah means to twist or whirl in a circular or spiraling manor; to fall grievously in pain or fear, to pervert, drive away, grieve, be sore pained, sorrowful, tremble, or wounded, a sandy dessert.[22] When I read these definitions it makes me think of all the spiraling out of control that has gone on in my own life, and in our culture and world. There are times in all our lives when sorrow and pain surround us. The strange thing is that Havilah was a land filled with gold, pearl, and onyx. Perhaps it is a description of all those who have great worldly wealth, but cannot seem to find peace or happiness in the center of their soul. Perhaps it speaks of western civilization that is so wealthy in creature comforts that their souls are starving to reconnect to their Creator.

Our providential turn of events is found in these Scriptures, but the extension of the mouth is our declaration of faith over our lives and the lives of others. When will we learn to let God be true and every man a liar? When will we learn our royal authority to declare and decree the Word of God over our lives and others' lives, to push back the gates of hell and find victory in living? Our confession of faith, our declaration of God's truth allows the living waters to bring peace into our lives. Circumstances may not change immediately, but we have a Father in heaven who holds us through each trial. And then we too can carry the truth of Christ's living waters into the lives of others. As you read these Scriptures write down what the Lord impresses on your heart.

Rev. 21:3-5

1Cor. 15:26

1Jhn. 5:12

1Cor. 15:54-57

1Co 15:22

Our words hold the power of life and death, choose life! May we be living water as we allow Jesus and His Spirit in us to encompass the whole land God has given us. Let us occupy and rescue the lost who have fallen in grievous pain or fear, which is what the land of Havilah represents. May we make a difference in the lives of those who live in a perverted land, have been driven away by the storms of life, and are grieved and sore pained by their pasts. Those that are wounded and trembling in a sandy dessert of the enemy's making need our Savior's love. May we grow in maturity in the Kingdom to help even one.

What stirred in your heart as you read about the river of Pishon and the land of Havilah?

THE RIVER OF GIHON IN THE LAND OF CUSH (ETHIOPIA)

The second river was Gihon and it flowed through the land of Cush, present day Ethiopia. Gihon simply means light that is bursting forth or gushing. The land of Cush means darkness or blackness.[23] In Genesis

1:2-3 we read *"The earth was formless and empty, and darkness covered the deep waters. And the Spirit of God was hovering over the surface of the waters. Then God said, "Let there be light," and there was light."* And in 2 Corinthians 4:6 *"For God, who said, "Let there be light in the darkness," has made this light shine in our hearts so we could know the glory of God that is seen in the face of Jesus Christ."* What a picture of creation bursting forth in light and the spiritual experience of having Christ shine in our hearts. This second river depicts the river of light flowing from the throne of God into us, bursting forth into a dark world. We are the light of the world, just like Jesus, as He forms His image in us. This land and its people are described in 2 Timothy 3:2-5. Read those verses.

- When it says 'a form of godliness but denying its power' what power is it referring to?

> *"Then the LORD said to Moses, "Stretch out your hand toward the sky so that darkness spreads over Egypt— darkness that can be felt." So Moses stretched out his hand toward the sky, and total darkness covered all Egypt for three days. No one could see anyone else or move about for three days. Yet all the Israelites had light in the places where they lived"* (Ex. 10:21-23).

The darkness of the land of Cush is like this. It is a shroud of the enemy's making that subverts life and cloaks truth. It is a darkness that separates its inhabitant from light, until God makes a way where there seems to be no way, until God pierces that darkness with the light of His Truth. It says in Psalm 139:12 *"…even the darkness will not be dark to you; the night will shine like the day, for darkness is as light to you."* The darkness is as light to Him, because He sees all regardless of the depth of darkness and knows all things. He reveals truth and life to his people.

Even darkness is as light to us as well, as we keep our spirit connected to His. His light in us can pierce any darkness.

- Have there been times in your life when you have sensed God's light in the midst of darkness?

"You are all children of the light and children of the day. We do not belong to the night or to the darkness. So then, let us not be like others, who are asleep, but let us be awake and sober" (1 Thess. 5:5-6).

- How can we awake and be sober (for or against what)?

"Arise, shine, for your light has come, and the glory of the LORD rises upon you. See, darkness covers the earth and thick darkness is over the peoples, but the LORD rises upon you and his glory appears over you" (Isa. 60:1-2). .

- What are some ways we can let our light shine?

"The city does not need the sun or the moon to shine on it, for the glory of God gives it light, and the Lamb is its lamp. The nations will walk by its light, and the kings of the earth will bring their splendor into it. On no day will its gates ever be shut, for there will be no night there" (Rev. 21:23-25).

Oh what a glorious day that will be! But for now, Jesus calls us to be the light in this dark land of Cush. We cannot impact every corner of this earth, but we can take the land where our feet tread.

- What areas of this dark world is Jesus calling you to impact? Remember even a cup of water given in His name will be rewarded.

I don't know about you, but I never liked the dark. I do not mind a moon lit night, but total darkness is quite another matter. Our world is getting darker day by day spiritually, and the things we were shocked at in the 50's and 60's are now common place. Filth is displayed daily on television screens, and the riots and violence in our cities and nations is many times incomprehensible. The enemy lulled many into accepting immorality little by little, until light and darkness in our culture are in stark contrast. Even though nothing is really new under the sun, we still fail to learn from generations past. From Genesis to today, sin has attempted to reign on the earth. Our mandate remains! Go and preach the gospel to all mankind, to every nation. As it gets darker, even the flicker of a candle can be seen from yards away. Stay connected to the light of Christ. Shine bright! Time seems short. Get up! Do the work of the ministry! As the river Gihon means light that is bursting forth or gushing, may we be a bursting light. May the fire of Holy Spirit baptize us with living fire we cannot contain as we share the Word with others. This land of Cush, this land of darkness has inhabitants full of fear and bondage crying for release from their chains. If you are born again and spirit filled, you have the authority and power in Christ to bring the light of Christ to many. Be bold! Be brave! Do not hold back. May Jesus find faith on the earth when He returns, and may each of us be the ones in which He finds that faith.

- How can you be a light in your home, workplace, church or community?

- Who is in darkness that you know who could use a phone call, a card, a text, an email or a visit today?

THE RIVER OF HIDDEKEL (TIGRIS) IN THE LAND OF ASHUR EAST OF ASSYRIA (SPIRITUAL BABYLON)

The third river that flowed from Eden was Hiddekel, current day Tigris, and flowed into the Land of Ashur. This Hiddekel River means rapid, lively, and full of life and swift running. This river was east, or in front and ahead, of all who dwell in Babylon. The Land of Ashur was bordered by Babylon and Assyria, which means successful.[24] This spiritual Babylonian area was a place of great success, but it was also a land of mixture. Assyrians were actually a mixture of the Babylonians and the Sumerians. They were also a people and land of great mixture of ideas, religions, and religious systems, indicative of the harlot that is successful due to being worldly-minded. We must be careful to distinguish between the *systems* of Babylon and the *captives* of Babylon.

- Define the systems of Babylon?

- Who do you think are the captives of Babylon in regards to religious systems?

I think one of the most sobering Scriptures in the Word is Matthew 7:22-23. *"Many will say to me on that day, 'Lord, Lord, did we not prophesy in your name and in your name drive out demons and in your name perform many miracles?' Then I will tell them plainly, 'I never knew you. Away from me, you evildoers'!"*

Many today are living in the mixture of this world and the Kingdom of God. They will one day stand before King Jesus and hear those words. God have mercy. May we not be among them; choose this day whom you will serve! It is a daily choice, and we cannot mix our affections with the things of this world. In Daniel ten, specifically verse four, we read an account of Daniel who was standing on the edge of the Tigris River and received a revelation from the Lord about future events. If we find ourselves in the land of Ashur today, that land of mixture, may we stand and receive from the waters of life a revelation of God's love and desire. May we be still long enough to hear His voice. May we see visions and learn to recognize the heart of God.

- Read the account of Daniel in chapters 10-11. Have you or anyone you know encountered God in a dynamic way? If so, share. If not, do you think this is possible today?

- Has a 'religious spirit' ever captured your heart over intimacy with Christ?

Just as this Hiddekel River meant rapid, lively, full of life and swift running, so too must be the Spirit of the living God within us. As we face a culture of mixture it is so easy to be deceived. We must not be deceived or be double minded in this precious life we have been given. We cannot have mixture in our own lives. If anything is more important than Christ in our lives, we need to prioritize our relationship with God, and know that sitting at Jesus' feet is the better thing. As we connect to the source of all life, we too will be a rapid, lively, and full of life. We will be a swift running river in our world. Our world is one of peoples and cultures of great mixture of ideas, religions, and religious systems that need the abundance of the living waters of Jesus Christ. May we seek Jesus daily with our whole heart, mind and soul to be ready for the great harvest of souls in the land in these times.

What action do you feel the Lord asking you to take at this point in your life?

THE RIVER OF EUPHRATES / THE LAND OF FERTILITY

The fourth river Euphrates, the fertile river, means to make fruitful, grow, increase, to break forth or rushing. It runs in a fertile land.[25] My take on this is that His Spirit flows into fertile areas of the remnant church of Jesus Christ and will continue into eternity. The Lord does not just refresh the lands of sorrow and grief, the lands of blackness and darkness, and the lands of religious systems and Babylonian mixture, but He certainly refreshes His own people to grow and produce fruit in and through their lives. But we as individuals must first traverse our own lands of sorrows, darkness and mixture before God's power is released through us.

Reread Ezekiel 47:1-12 and meditate on this Scripture that was taught on in an earlier chapter. I pray you see the significance of it more now. I pray we move in the river of His presence all the days of our lives. I love that this river means not only fruitfulness and growth, but a breaking forth or rushing. Oh, that the Spirit of God would break forth in this Third Great Awakening as a mighty river rushing through our families, cities, nation and world until the last one hears the gospel of Truth.

> *The desert and the parched land will be glad; the wilderness will rejoice and blossom. Like the crocus, it will burst into bloom; it will rejoice greatly and shout for joy. The glory of Lebanon will be given to it, the splendor of Carmel and Sharon; they will see the glory of the LORD, the splendor of our God. The burning sand will become a pool, the thirsty ground bubbling springs. In the haunts*

where jackals once lay, grass and reeds and papyrus will grow. ... No lion will be there, nor any ravenous beast; they will not be found there. But only the redeemed will walk there" (Isa 35:1-2, 7, 9).

- Into all the lands we looked at, what is prophesied here?

"For this is what the Lord has commanded us: "I have made you a light for the Gentiles, that you may bring salvation to the ends of the earth" (Acts 13:47).

- Why do you think we sometimes take the Word as a suggestion and not a command?

"God made him who had no sin to be sin for us, so that in him we might become the righteousness of God" (2 Cor. 5:21).

- When we feel unworthy, incapable, or unprepared what must we remember?

Read the following Scriptures and answer the questions:
Read Isaiah 49:6.

- What promise can we declare from this Scripture?

Read Jeremiah 17:5-8, 13.

- What has been bothering you or worrying you lately?

- Define trust.

- How can we better make the LORD our hope and confidence?

Read 2 Chronicles. 20:15.

- Would you agree that sometimes we feel it is our battle? How can we surrender that thinking to the Lord?

Read Jeremiah 9:24.

May you flow in Holy Spirit empowered spiritual life as His life flows through you to a thirsty world. The Lord even now prepares a RIVER OF LIFE PEOPLE to flow into the whole land of death (Havilah), into the whole land of darkness (Ethiopia), into the whole land of spiritual Babylon (Assyria), and into His Precious Bride the Church.

So, are you ready to take up your new sword, your new mantle, your new commission? God has great things in store for those who trust in Him. As His children, our Father is asking us to put on our battle boots, fasten our armor, pick up our shield and sword and walk bravely and confidently into the next season of our life until He returns. The road may be rocky, the conditions sorrowful, the darkness intense, and the deception increasing, but He promised us a harvest of souls in the last days. I, for one, will take Him at His Word. Jesus is our source, our substance, our goal! He is our all in all! May He be praised all the days of our lives! Let's bring Him glory!

#12. Our last obstacle may be deception and the inability or unwillingness to "Get Up!" May these not keep us from enjoying a right relationship with the Father as His son or daughter in these last days. I pray there are no more obstacles keeping us from the destiny written of us in the books of heaven. In every previous chapter I have engaged you in thinking about the obstacles that keep us from accepting not only Abba's love but also standing up in obedience to His call. There may have been some obstacles in your life that kept you from believing you can be God's son or daughter, or seeing with your spiritual eyes His great love for you. Those obstacles included:

1. Sin or guilt because you had not come to Jesus in repentance and given your all to Him.
2. Constantly wandering from God in disobedience
3. The enemy's accusations that you are not worthy or enough
4. Your fear of rejection from others or a Holy God
5. Doubts and fears
6. Thinking you have abandoned all to Christ but haven't
7. The crushing weight of brokenness
8. The fear of the Supernatural
9. Remembering our righteousness is as filthy rags
10. Finding security in this Kingdom realm
11. Boasting in something or someone other than Christ
12. Deception or unwillingness to "Get Up"

And now you may ask, "Who Me?" Remember that you are His child, and He has given you a new sword, everything you need for life and godliness. I pray we have laid down every obstacle at Messiah's feet. Cross out the ones above you now have victory over. Commit to finding victory in each of the other areas. Together let us declare this final prayer:

Prayer to 'Or Goyim, A Light to the Nations

I declare and decree that every bondage and obstacle in my life is shattered and lay under my feet. I declare and decree that my sin and guilt are covered by the Blood of the Lamb, and the enemy of my soul has no accusation against me. I declare and decree that disobedience and wandering from my Father's love no longer have authority over my mind, for Jesus is transforming me into His image and I have the mind of Christ. I declare and decree that the fears within have been silenced, because Jesus has not given me a spirit of fear but of power, and love, and a sound mind. I declare and decree that I no longer fear rejections, because I am crucified with Christ and the life I now live is no longer mine but His, and He accepts me as I am. I declare and decree that doubts and fears have no hold on me, because they are the enemy's tools to debilitate my call and authority in the land. I declare and decree that when I do not abandon all to the cause of Christ, that His Spirit will rise up within me, even in my weakness, to advance the Kingdom. I declare and decree that the crushing weight of brokenness will no longer have a hold on my life, for I have been conformed to the suffering of Christ, and no student is above their teacher. Jesus has risen from the dead and so shall I. I declare and decree that I will have no fear of the supernatural lifestyle, for it is my inheritance in the Kingdom of God for all eternity so walking in it is both my call and joy. I declare and decree that Holy Spirit will cause me to keep a humble heart, and remember that my righteousness is as filthy rags. I declare and decree that I will not find my security in the realm of this world, but only in the realm of my heavenly Father. I declare and decree that I will not boast in any other shield or banner, but my boast is only in the righteousness of Jesus Christ. I declare and decree that as I open my mouth, God will fill it. I can speak truth into the atmosphere and demons will flee. I can speak the Word and enemies will scatter. I declare and decree that the destiny written of me in the books of heaven will be fulfilled in the earth. I declare and decree Jesus has shod my feet with the gospel of peace, and many will come to salvation because of my obedience to the call. I declare and decree that I will not be deceived, but get up each time my Lord calls. **'Or Goyim, A Light to the Nations** I hold strong and steady the shield of faith and proclaim the great works that God has done. I pick up my sword, the Word of God, and take the land before me in the name that surpasses every other name, Jesus the Christ, my Living Lord. Amen.

I am praying for you sweet sons and daughters of the Most High God. Be brave and wield your sword with boldness and authority. Reread the prayer 'A New Sword for My Bride' at the beginning of this book and commit to praying for Christ's Church, His precious Bride.

Poetry of Grace

Let my soul sing a love song
And my worship be my life
Let my heart belong to only Thee
'Till each fragment, truly free

Helping souls know your cadence
Releasing captives from this world
May their hearts know your presence
'Till we're one- Your very essence

Let our souls release Your glory
Each hour, time, and place
Let our hearts no longer be our own
'Till church and Bride be fully grown

Every soul, heaven's aroma
Its fragrance permeating senses
Let all hearts no longer be fractured
'Till Your presence be our eternal rapture

ACKNOWLEDGMENTS

First and foremost I wish to thank my Abba Father for making a way where there seemed to be no way. I thank Jesus Christ for being my Lord and Savior. I thank Holy Spirit for never giving up on me. I thank my Triune God for the miracle of life, this abundant life, eternal life and the joy He orchestrates for me in the poetry of grace.

Sincere thanks to my dear husband, Terry, who has always supported and encouraged me in the Lord's work. Love, blessings and thanks to my precious children for putting up with me all these years as God was working on my heart. Thanks also to my special 'Jesus Family' who prays for me through thick and thin, and who encourage me with prayer, laughter and love: Bonnie, Al, Marianne, Brad, Cyndi, Fred, Nancy T., Paul, Nancy K., Sharon, Mark, Tracey, Arnie, Lynn, Doug, Alyce, Jeff, and Cheryl.

I would also like to acknowledge the beautiful painting of Robert Stover, my husband's maternal grandfather and Barbara Dalton, my husband's sister. Their paintings were used in the beginning of two of the chapters. Thanks also to the creative design work of Lydia, a special young lady, who helped with the graphic design of one of my revelations of God's love; the four rivers.

This effort would not have been completed without all the children of God who have captured my heart, and the pastors and teachers who shared Christ's love with me. To all God's sons and daughters who have seized Christ's heart, may they partner their story with Jesus' beautiful salvation message. Thanks to all the people who have continued to captivate my heart in their stories, laughter, tears and fellowship: in my family, my church, my career, my home groups, at the prison, in the streets, and throughout my life. They are why I write; may their sorrows be fewer, their joys multiplied, and their victories many.

REFERENCES / RECOMMENDED READING

Focus on the Family, *The Truth Project DVD Set* (Colorado Springs, CO: Focus of the Family, 2006).

Henri T. Blackaby, Richard Blackaby, Claude V. King, *Experiencing God: Knowing and Doing the Will of God* (Nashville, TN: Lifeway, 2007).

Josh McDowell, Sean McDowell, PhD, *Evidence That Demands a Verdict: Life-Changing Truth for a Skeptical World* (Nashville, TN: Thomas Nelson, 2017).

Joyce Meyer, *Battlefield of the Mind* (New York, NY: Hachette Book Group Inc., 2017).

Rick Renner, *Dressed to Kill: A Biblical Approach to Spiritual Warfare and Armor* (Tulsa, OK: Harrison House Publishers, 1991).

Robert Henderson, *Accessing the Courts of Heaven: How to Position Yourself for Breakthrough* Prayer (Shippensburg, PA: Destiny Image, 2017).

R.T. Kendall, *Holy Fire: A Balance Look at the Holy Spirit's Work in Our Lives* (Lake Mary, FL: Charisma House, 1984).

Sandie Freed, *Destiny Thieves: Defeat Seducing Spirits and Achieve Your Purpose* (Grand Rapids, MI: Chosen Books a division of Baker Publishing Group, 2007).

Smith Wigglesworth, *Smith Wigglesworth on Manifesting the Power of God* (Shippensburg, PA: Destiny Image, 2016).

ABOUT THE AUTHOR

Judith Loeper is a compassionate poet, writer and communicator of the Word of God. She has been married to her husband Terry for 43 years and has two grown children. She enjoys gardening, puzzles, reading and serving in the Kingdom. Her passion is to influence others to truly encounter freedom in Christ. Judy graduated from Clarion University with a Bachelor's degree in Special Education. She attended Millersville University, receiving her Master's in Education in 1981. She taught students K-9 with emotional needs for sixteen years, and then taught third and fourth grade for nineteen additional years. She did doctoral work in Administrative Supervision at Immaculata University until 2004. She received her K-12 Principle Certification from Alvernia University in 2004. She is a credentialed Minister through Christian Global Outreach Ministries, and has been ordained an independent Christian clergy to perform any and all Christian religious services, ministerial and evangelical duties. She currently serves with Revelation 19 Ministries team with Evangelist Tracey Weiss. She has served on several mission trips both in the states and abroad. Judy has served in ministry over her lifetime in various capacities including: Worship Team, Choir, Home Bible Studies, Women's Ministries and Councils, Prison Ministry, Street Ministry, Healing Ministry, Mentoring Trainings and Altar Ministry. She has witnessed multiple miracles and salvations, and prays for the multitudes to be set free from every bondage for all eternity by following Jesus Christ.

"The secret things belong to the LORD our God, but the things revealed belong to us and to our children forever, that we may follow all the words of this law" (Deut. 29:29).

ENDNOTES

CHAPTER ONE

[1] Tony Evans, *Praying Through the Names of God* (Eugene, Ore.: Harvest House Publishers, 2014).

[2] Steven Curtis Chapman, *Glorious Unfolding*, Producer Steven Curtis Chapman and Brent Milligan, 2013.

[3] Oswald Chambers, *My Utmost for His Highest*, (Nashville, TN: Thomas Nelson Publishers, 1995), Nov. 30.

[4] Dr. David Jeremiah, *Captured By Grace* (Nashville, TN: Thomas Nelson, 2010).

[5] Focus on the Family, *The Truth Project* (Colorado Springs, CO: Focus of the Family, 2006).

CHAPTER TWO

[6] Henri Nouwen, *Further Reflections on the Parable of the Prodigal Son* (New York City, NY: Random House, 2002).

[7] Rueben Job, *Wesleyan Spiritual Reader* (Nashville, TN: Abingdon Press, 1997).

CHAPTER THREE

8 Henri T. Blackaby, Richard Blackaby, Claude V. King, *Experiencing God: Knowing and Doing the Will of God* (Nashville, TN: Lifeway, 2007).

CHAPTER FIVE

9 Josh McDowell, Sean McDowell, PhD, *Evidence That Demands a Verdict: Life-Changing Truth for a Skeptical World* (Nashville, TN: Thomas Nelson, 2017).

10 Max Lucado, *Grace for the Moment: Inspirational Thoughts for Each Day of the Year* (Nashville, TN: Thomas Nelson, 2000).

11 Robert Henderson, *Accessing the Courts of Heaven: How to Position Yourself for Breakthrough Prayer* (Shippensburg, PA: Destiny Image, 2017).

CHAPTER SEVEN

12 C.H. Spurgeon, *Spurgeon's Quotes: The Definitive Collection* (Woodlands, TX: Kress Christian Publications, 2018).

13 Oswald Chambers, *My Utmost for His Highest* (Special Updated Edition) (Grand Rapids, MI: Discovery House Publishers, 1995).

CHAPTER NINE

14 David Wilkerson, *It is Finished: Finding Lasting Victory Over Sin* (Ada, MI: Chosen Books, 2013).

CHAPTER ELEVEN

15 James Strong, *The New Strong's Exhaustive Concordance of the Bible* (Nashville, TN: Thomas Nelson Publishers, 1984), ref. no. 4268.

[16] Ibid., ref. no. 4309.

[17] Ibid., ref. no. 4964.

[18] Ibid., ref. no. H7121.

[19] Ibid., ref. no. G1344.

[20] Ibid., ref. no. G1392.

CHAPTER TWELVE

[21] Ibid., ref. no. H5731.

[22] Ibid., ref. nos. H6376 & H 2341.

[23] Ibid., ref. nos. H1521 & H3568.

[24] Ibid., ref. nos. H2313 & H806.

[25] Ibid., ref. nos. H6578 & H1568.

CPSIA information can be obtained
at www.ICGtesting.com
Printed in the USA
BVHW090207120822
644423BV00004B/8